BRODART, CO.   Cat. No. 23-221-003

ORIGINAL SIX

True Stories from Hockey's Classic Era

Edited by
PAUL QUARRINGTON

REED
BOOKS
CANADA

This edition first published in Canada by
Reed Books Canada
204 Richmond Street West
Suite 300
Toronto Ontario
M5V 1V6

Canadian Cataloguing in Publication Data

Main entry under title:

Original six: true stories from hockey's classic era

ISBN 0–433–39752–7

1. National Hockey League – History.   2. Hockey – History.
3. Hockey players.   I. Quarrington, Paul.

GV847.8.N3075   1996   796.962'06   C95–933250–2

Printed in Canada

Design and page composition: Andrew Smith Graphics Inc.

Copy-editing: Peggy McKee

CONTENTS

INTRODUCTION

BY PAUL QUARRINGTON

THERE IS A BLIGHT UPON THE LAND. I DON'T MEAN TO BE alarming, but there you go. Besides, it's not a major blight, it's only a bit of a blight, a blightette. You may well have noted the signs without their truly registering.

For example: A crowd sits in a tavern, half a dozen television sets suspended from the walls. Across the screens float the images of hockey players. The jerseys bear the names of distant U.S. cities. The men play with a workmanlike intensity and the tavern dwellers respond only to fights and goals. For each the reaction is the same, a pugnacious and vindictive punching of the air.

What's missing, of course, is real enthusiasm. On both sides.

There is a blight (at least a blighteenie) upon the land.

A few years ago, a hockey player got into trouble for a strange transgression: washing his sports car at midnight without any pants on. As a veteran sportswriter mused, "Oh, my goodness, what passes for colour these days!"

A blight-lite upon the land. The ice stadia are empty and quiet. The wintry streets are deserted. There are very few people who water their lawns in mid-January any more (summoning from the night an irregular, bumpy and altogether perfect backyard rink), afraid to ruin the grass that will come with the spring.

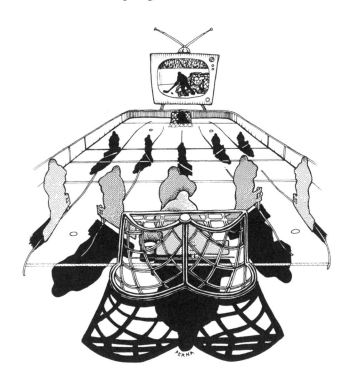

☆ INTRODUCTION ☆

I'm not mourning the passing of the good old days. I'm lamenting the lack of good days, period.

This book isn't nostalgic. It's analeptic. Which is to say, we mean it to be a restorative.

It is not about the six franchises, not really. It is about enthusiasm.

Dave Bidini (whose story here was supposed to be about the Chicago Blackhawks but is really about heaven) knows something about enthusiasm. Just the other autumnal day I asked him how he was. "Oh, stiff," he complained. "I'm playing hockey again."

"But you played all summer," I pointed out.

"Oh, yeah," he admitted, "but that was just once a week."

Bidini is, like the men who populate his story about the tragic Charlie Gardiner, *god-awful in love with the game*. He is in love with the actual practice of it (which he executes with a kind of loping grace that belies his status as rock star — the rhythm guitarist for the Rheostatics); he is in love with the history; he is in love with the stories. We exchange the stories, he and I, on those long wintry nights when no one seems to be able to muster much in the way of enthusiasm, when the teams from distant U.S. cities on the suspended television screens are playing sound defensive hockey (and let me remind you that the sow bug's strategy of rolling itself up into a little armoured booger is sound, defensively). Exchanging these stories works for us, and the

7

hope is that it will work for you, a balm for the blightette.

We decided to have six stories, which had a pleasing resonance because there were at one point only six teams, or perhaps because of the Original Six we decided on six stories. It doesn't much matter. In choosing the other writers I tended to go for emotional rightness over historical expertise. I recalled something written by Wayne Johnston (whose story was supposed to be about the Montreal Canadiens and the St. Patrick's Day riot but is instead about conviction). In Johnston's novel *The Divine Ryans* a character rhapsodizes about Bobby Hull's slapshot, explaining that the shot was so hard and fast that it actually went *back in time*. Bobby Hull's slapshots were affecting the outcome of games played years ago.

Yeah, I thought, that's the ticket.

I recalled a poet named Judith Fitzgerald, how she was a huge baseball fan, the author of an article about opening day that contained a sentence of great eloquence and beauty, a koan for the sports fan. On opening day, Fitz had written, "All heaven breaks out." I wondered if she was at all interested in hockey and arranged a meeting. She was a fanatic about baseball, true, but in a sense that game was just something to do between hockey seasons. Her story was supposed to be about the Detroit Red Wings and Gordie Howe's near-fatal accident, but it is really about the fragility, and the great strength, of family.

☆ INTRODUCTION ☆

Bidini and I realized, at some point, that many of the stories we told each other had the same fount. There is a chronicler of hockey's heroic and comic, a Homer for all the shinny men. Indeed, my story (which is supposed to be about Eddie Shore and, come to think of it, is) has as its source *The Mad Men of Hockey,* by Trent Frayne. Frayne was contacted, engaged and convinced to throw away a lifetime's habit of writing factually accurate and incontrovertible prose. "Write us a little fiction," I advised him. "Just make sure it's true." His story was supposed to be about the Toronto Maple Leafs and the impish King Clancy but is instead about that inconstant companion, memory.

Bidini had met Jeff Klein in New York City, where Klein edited the sports section for the *Village Voice.* (That newspaper no longer has one; a blight upon the land!) His story was supposed to be about the New York Rangers and their finally drinking from the Stanley Cup, but it is really about the fall from grace and redemption.

It was Bidini who knew the artists, Sean Thompson and Frank Perna, because he travels across the land and meets like-minded (read: hockey-obsessed) people. Their work is beautiful, but don't take my word for it, flip through and have a gander your own self.

Others that need to be thanked: Sean Luxton, Peter Goddard, Dean Cooke and Oliver Saltzmann.

1

THE CHICAGO BLACKHAWKS

BY DAVE BIDINI

Style —go ahead talking about style
You can tell where a man got his style just
 as you can tell where Pavlova got her legs
 or Ty Cobb his batting eye

 Go on talking.
Only don't take my style away
 It's my face.
 Maybe no good
 But anyway, my face.
I talk with it, sing with it, I see, taste and
 feel with it, I know why I want to keep it.

CARL SANDBURG

Charles Gardiner

☆

Children, there is no Loop in heaven. There are no cities like Chicago, Illinois, built along a vertebra of steelwork with a skyline that looks like it was dreamed up by giants in double-breasted suits chewing cigars and jangling pocket change. There's no *nrrggh,* no grinding of gears, no soldiering of citizenry through the streets, no rioting of trumpets, no confetti spilling out of bags upended from city windows, no yowling cabbies or pug schoolkids, no stink, no din, no nothin'. Heaven is like a resort, a big, friggin' HoJo's. It's all right for fellas dead from black lung who spent their lives mining in East Bumhole, Ontario, but for me, Charlie Gardiner, give me my dirty old city home, give me the el train that shoots over the street and shakes the countertop of the diner that serves strong black coffee and good cheesecake. These sunny vistas and hanging gardens and half-dressed nubiles waving palm fronds, these velvety paintings come alive, they bore me stiff. Look, there's Bing Crosby. Bing I call Captain Ennui. He likes the name. He sits around in his yachtsman's hat and sweater singing and humming all day then tricks me into playing checkers with him. I hate friggin' checkers.

A few huts down the beach, Renoir paints feverishly, making lovely stuff, but he produces so much of it, so often, that when he runs up to you on the beach with his canvas and yells, "Look at *zis* masterpiece!" and it's no better or worse than the one he did the day before, you get the feeling of *same old, same old*. Caruso, the Italian tenor, is my other neighbour. If he moved down the beach and his place was taken by a bean counter, I would not miss him at all. I used to love the opera, but now I'm sick of it. I also used to love hockey until I played in heaven, in a game where everyone threw a clean check, scored a pretty goal and made a great play that saved the friggin' day, which is fine if you like shooting fish in a barrel.

But give me the *nrrggh*. Back in the 1930s, when I squared the pipes and captained the team for the Blackhawks of Illinois, back when Lord Stanley's chalice was no bigger than a piss pot, being a hockey player was something else. Of course, the conditions were less than perfect, and you know that if the people in charge up here ever tried to re-create what it was like to be a hockey player during the Depression, they'd try to smooth out all the imperfections, which probably explains why all of those miners walk around with perfect teeth and talk like Leslie friggin' Howard.

In the 1930s, arenas were cramped, cold and smokey, and the players were helmetless, underpaid hellions, exploited by the owners then spit out of the league with nothing to show for their service but a rank bag of equipment. But they also lived a charmed life. To a man they were proud, tough and god-awful in love with the game. And back then, Saturday night in six cities was an event like the opera or the circus, right on down from the grizzly gin-pickled poets of press row to the gowned ladies of state and their money lords, who sat rinkside in box seats wearing white gloves.

Up in the cheap seats, thugs chanted like Piltdown man, their voices raining upon us in the worst of times like fish emptied from a great barrel. A few times a year, every year, they descended from the bleachers and jumped the boards to get at us like they were part of the game. The fans hated us hard, but they loved us harder. And we gave it right back.

I once had 500 fans chase me around the Loop in the Windy City while "Broadway" Roger Jenkins rolled me around in a wheelbarrow, his payment for losing a bet. See, Jenkins, the muggins, wagered midseason that we would not beat Detroit if we played them in the finals, which we did, and we bettered them three games to one. I'd say, and you could stamp it, that that day in the Loop was the happiest day of my life. As I recall, light snow had coated the sides of the el stations faster than the spring sun could melt it. Poor Jenkins was a terrible bucket driver, so when the wheelbarrow hiccupped over sewer grates and trolley tracks, the bucket tipped side to side and a couple of times I nearly fell out. Washerwomen and housewives and city workers were hanging out of windows cheering us on, waving hankies. Cars and taxis *phlanged!* their horns. Cops ran alongside us, slapping our backs and grabbing our hands to shake them. I could hear Jenkins laughing like a clown as he raced to stay just in front of the surging crowd. I plugged my fedora down over my brow, stuffed my hands deep inside my overcoat and chewed on a heater. Those were the good times.

Children, let me crack a Coke and tell you about them.

I am a goaltender. I am also a singer. They used to let me sing on the radio in Winnipeg, Manitoba, back when I was something of a star attraction on the prairies. In truth, I couldn't tell whether or not listeners actually tuned in for the music or whether they treasured hearing an actual National Hockey League player make a muck of himself over the bright lights of the round dial. Whatever the case, my singing was my therapy, and it used to scare the living bejesus out of the visiting team when I'd burst into song as the puck was tied up behind the net or along the side boards. Bloody Eddie Shore of the Boston Bruins would try to get the ref to penalize me for this (Shore thought of every way to gain an advantage), but instead of giving me a pair for obstruction, the zebras would even request the odd tune. That drove Shore nuts.

"You fat little turd." He'd skate by me and scowl.

"I'm in the mood for love, simply because you're near me ..."

"C'mere, I'll stick this fuckin' blade in ya. Cut you a new cornhole."

"... funny but when you're near me ..."

"You wait, Gardiner. You're mine, you friggin' bastard."

"... ah, I'm in the mood for love."

Like I said, I am a goaltender. I don't expect all of you to be impressed by that. If you don't follow the game of hockey or if you've never seen a game, you could easily mistake a goaltender for the scouse outside the rink selling whirligigs and candy corn. To a man, we're paunchy lummoxes who seem better suited to plumb your john than thwart the great skating golden boys of our time. Woefully, we don't look like much at all. Only goaltenders find other goalies decent looking. The last men with whom the women in the bar ever want to dance are the goalies, the pachyderms of the sporting world, slow and heavy, one rung above the punter. Besides, our job was created in the early days of the game because the object of the sport — to put the biscuit between the markers — became too easy. The goaltender was born to make what the rest of the players do more difficult. It's a wonder we haven't been drummed from the sport and replaced by a bucket with a buzzer.

When I first started skating as a pup fresh off the boat from Scotland, I saw myself pirouetting across the great ice surfaces of the world's stage or winding like a water snake through the league's all-star squads. I give you my word, I never imagined throwing my body in front of flying chunks of frozen rubber, pucks thunking off my skull. But we all know what happened. Because I was a late bloomer, the other neighbourhood boys were advanced in the skills department, so when choosing squads for shinny, I was usually left behind with the weaker kids, some of whom didn't even have skates.

Team captains would look at us and say, "And of the dregs we have left, who wants to step inside the nets and take their licking?" Since I wanted to play so badly, my hand went up like a flag. Before I knew it, I was standing keeled over the bathroom sink, my body aching and battered like bruised fruit, my teeth snapping off like Chiclets into my mouth. In my first game as a goalie, I froze outside for three hours with nothing but schoolbooks strapped to my knees for protection. I shivered in the crease and I took it; I took everything those terrible scamps had to offer. What kind of a muggins was I that I stood there and loved it?

When my family and I came to Canada from Edinburgh, Scotland, in 1911, we travelled for two weeks in the nocturnal hull of a great steamship, third-class steerage, Scotland's shoreline disappearing behind us like a curling stone sliding off the edge of the Earth. When the ship finally docked in North America and made its expulsion, the scene on shore was something I'll never forget. The dock was swarming with people running and shouting and gesturing wildly, a maelstrom of noise and colour and strange faces. The men wore hats, the women kerchiefs, their bodies scrummaged together in wool and linen, crying out to friends and relatives. Somewhere in there my father pulled his family through the crowd, uphill to the train station to continue our journey toward Winnipeg.

This same crowd would stare back at me years later from the arena stands in my days as a Blackhawk. Out of that scene came the faces of the men and women who would hold up autograph pads for me to sign after games, who'd slap our backs in hotel bars and shake our hands and buy us drinks and try to bribe us, who'd deal us into card games on trains and hand out cigars and expound on the secrets of their industries, who'd sell us handpicked apples and berries at city markets, who'd fill our automobiles with gas and wash our windshields, who'd tailor our suits, resole our shoes, block our hats, trim our ducktails, sweep our doorways. I saw these people in every arena in North America. I was drawn to them. I started talking to them during games.

"Hey, Charlie! How're ya feeling tonight?"

"Fresh as an Annapolis daisy in the Ottawa Valley, pal!"

"Hey, Chuck, how do the Wings look to ya?"

"Like they maybe wished they'd never laid eyes on the likes of us!"

"Hey, Mr. Gardiner. Can you say hi to my girl?"

"No. But I'll dedicate save Number 12 to her, a glove save, a pretty one, top corner. When are you two gonna get married, anyhow?"

"As soon as you guys win the Cup!"

"I was afraid you'd say that!"

The crowd would erupt in laughter.

When's the last time you heard anyone laugh at a hockey game?

My greatest season as a Chicago Blackhawk was 1933–34. Since being purchased from the Winnipeg Maroons in 1927, I had become something of a local celebrity around the Windy City for my colourful play. Before I came to Chicago, the only road trip I'd taken out of Manitoba was the time one of our peewee coaches hired a couple of horse-drawn sleighs to take us to a game on the Saskatchewan border, where we played on an ice rink lit by torches hung at either end of the ice above the goals.

So when I got to the Big Smoke, it was like I'd discovered Mecca, and I made the most of my time there. And while I didn't drink or carry on, I could still kick it up with the best of them. The boys and I would go to the Bismarck Hotel, a wonderful building with high glassy ceilings and walls and balconies inlaid with purple stone and gold trim, beautiful classical tapestries draping fine smoking rooms, tuxedoed waiters working their long oak bars and gorgeous, lamplit ballrooms designed for their great bands, led by Fletcher Henderson, Count Basie and others. The Capone clan used to go there, and so did the theatre and movie people, as well as Cubbie and White Stocking ballplayers and the odd cop or councilman on the make.

We behaved like we never could in Brandon, Manitoba, Sudbury, Ontario, or Salmon Arm, British Columbia. It was at the Bismarck where I once danced with Hollywood starlet Myrna Loy. The boys back home pissed themselves when I wrote them about that one. What I didn't tell them was what happened when Ms. Loy inquired as to what I did for a living. I told her that I was a hockey player, that I was the league-leading goalkeeper for the Chicago Blackhawks.

"No. No, really." She laughed, holding a drink

"That's all there is, ma'am," I insisted.

"Well then, what's your name, dear?"

"Charlie, Charlie Gardiner."

"Hmmm. Sorry, never heard of you."

The 1933–34 hockey season was strange. It started weird and got weirder. The first episode of import was when Eddie Shore refused to report to the Boston Bruins unless they did something about his salary; namely, raise it. And although hockey players had done that kind of thing before, we were in a Depression at the time, and the players were eager to see what Shore could squeeze out of Charles Adams, the Bruins' skinflint owner. As it turned out, Shore was promptly back in the league on November 14 for a game against the Montreal Canadiens. He'd signed for the league's highest salary — $7,500 — right there in front of

NHL president Frank Calder at Bonaventure station in Montreal, Quebec, on a beautiful autumn afternoon. He told reporters later that since he was worth so much money, he was adopting a gentler style of hockey to prolong his career. When Lionel "Big Train" Conacher heard that, he said to me in the Pullman, "Yeah, and I'm Gypsy Rose Lee." And he was right, because once the season got under way, Shore didn't go any softer.

On December 12, 1933, at a game against the Toronto Maple Leafs in the Garden in Boston, Massachusetts, Shore showed why he was still the nastiest s.o.b. who ever spit teeth. That was the night he put Irvine "Ace" Bailey out of hockey. Shore hit Bailey from behind during a stop in play and sent him high in the air and then face first back into the ice. His head was cracked at both temples, blood streaming down his face and neck as he was pulled limp as a pup from the ice. They worked on Bailey tirelessly that night, and legend has it that he was so close to death that Conn Smythe, the Leafs' inscrutable owner, had made arrangements to transport his dead body back to Toronto, Ontario, in the morning. How Bailey ever survived that horrible night in Beantown I'll never know.

Apparently, while Bailey was unconscious and being examined by the team doctor in the infirmary, he suddenly awoke spry as a robin and looked at his coach, Dick Irvin, and said, "Put me back in the game, Dick. The fellas need me." Minutes later, when Shore came in with Art Ross, the Bruins' coach and general manager, and saw that Bailey's noggin was blood-soaked and bandaged like a mummy's, Shore leaned over to Bailey and apologized for the hit, at which point he sat up, smiled and said, "It's okay, Eddie. It's all part of the game." The little man got all goofy at death's door. Something about that I like.

The deed was finally squared when Shore and Bailey shook hands and embraced a few months later at a game in which a team of NHLers, myself included, played the Leafs in what turned out to be the league's very first all-star game, a fund-raiser to help pay for Bailey's medical bills. It was remarkable that something halfway good came out of such a terrible thing. When all was said and done, fans and players had raised $20,000, an incredible amount of money at the time. As you probably know, Bailey never played another game of professional hockey. Bloody Eddie Shore got five minutes for tripping.

The second important event in the hockey season of 1933–34 was the performance of the Chicago Blackhawks. We surprised everyone in the hockey world, and like I said before, even some fellas on our own team figured that Detroit had a lock on the Cup before anyone had played a single game. But something told me that we were due. Since Major Frederic McLaughlin, the general manager, had filled out the team at the beginning of the season by picking up Leroy Goldsworthy, Jack Leswick, the great Lionel Pretoria Conacher and a few misfits cast off by other clubs, at first we looked like a Keystone crew with only the smallest hope of scraping into the playoffs. To have seen a picture of us back then or to thumb down a team score sheet, you'd have thought that we looked old and uncompetitive. But on the ice we harmonized like no other team in the history of Blackhawk hockey.

I knew it would be a good year when, on December 19, Taffy Abel, our slow-footed sack-of-potatoes defenceman, scored his first goal in more than two years. It was a beauty, the puck bouncing and hiccupping about 50 times from the blueline through a forest of legs then leaping over the shoulder of the beleaguered goaltender of the hapless Ottawa Senators, a team in its death throes, playing accordingly. Abel fell to his knees like he'd been shot, whooped twice, then got up and jitterbugged to the bench like his ass was on fire. It was something to see, Abel so damned excited. Around the time of that game, we were in first place with an 11–7–6 record, so it was icing on the cake. We'd only scored 39 goals as a team, but I had surrendered just 28 in 24 games. As any scrub will tell you, you can't lose with those kinds of numbers. I finished the year with a 1.73 goals-against average and they gave me another Vézina Trophy to add to my collection.

In 1934, I could have won blindfolded. I stopped

everything that came my way. At the beginning of the season league officials had increased the size of the crease to eight by five feet, and it gave me a whole new domain in which to ply my trade. I stood on my head, flopped and danced around the net like a friggin' marionette on Georges Vézina's puppet strings. For the first half of the season, I felt quick and rubbery, my head 100 per cent into the game.

That came as a little bit of a surprise. See, in 1932, I had contracted the worst case of tonsillitis known to man, the kind where your tonsils swell up like billiard balls so that breathing is as tough as climbing the World Trade Center in cement sneakers. There were times that year when I couldn't move after games, when total convalescence was required between contests. On most days, I divided my time away from the rink between my home and the clinic, where doctors worked on finding a way to stop the swelling. I never missed a hockey game — not one — but my stubbornness did little to help the team's chances. We finished dead last that year and there were times when I thought the bastard had beaten me. The beginning of the 1933–34 season convinced me otherwise, but I hadn't seen the last of the devil malady; it very nearly robbed me of my greatest moment in hockey.

We had little Harold "Mush" March, five feet five inches, skittering up and down the ice like a water spider, threading passes to Doc Romnes and Rosie Couture; they could have hit a squirrel's ass with a cherry tomato the way they were shooting. We had Johnny Gottselig freezing defencemen like toy soldiers, then dropping the dot to Paul Thompson, who, along with Tommy Cook and Artie Coulter, made Swiss cheese out of opposing goalies. On defence, we had Conacher and Abel, swatting away the Frank Bouchers and Joe Primeaus of the league like they were horseflies. We were a great team led by a great man: Lionel Big Train Conacher, whose heartbeat sounded the loudest of all our players. When he came over to the Hawks in 1932, Coach Tommy Gorman made Conacher clean up his act, and you could see the change in him.

When I used to play against Conacher, he seemed foul and half-jarred. But after he got straight, well, I would have thrown myself in front of a friggin' locomotive for the guy. His face had taken more than 600 stitches and his nose had been broken four times. He was balding and a little on the wide side. But I've never laid eyes on an athlete quite like him. Baseball, rugby, football, you name it, he was a star at everything. Even in his 60s, years after quitting hockey, he was brilliant at sports. His death came on a baseball diamond during a charity game on Parliament Hill in Ottawa, Ontario, when he tried stretching a single into a triple. There's a famous picture of him standing safe at third base minutes before he collapsed, his shoulders proud and Olympian. It was behind these shoulders that we skated out against Detroit in Game 1 of the Stanley Cup Finals and were carried across them when we returned to Chicago with a shocking two-game lead.

By the time we came home, Chicago was jumping high as heaven for the underdog Hawks. On the train, the fellas were buzzing about the possibility of sweeping the Cup series in front of the hometown fans. Storefronts everywhere were painted with the Hawks logo; swing bands wrote songs like "The Blackhawk Stomp" and "Go, Charlie, Go!"; the mayor mentioned us every chance he got; restaurants added the Big Train Special to their menus; and garlands and boxes of chocolates and hand-knit sweaters and chicken soup and letters by the hundreds showed up at my door every morning during the playoffs. The city had gone Hawk-mad and the players could taste victory. All of Chicago's attention focused on Game 3, our first chance to put away the Wings and bring the city its very first Stanley Cup.

While all of this was going on, while the city strung huge banners across Wabash Avenue and Madison Street that roared Go Hawks Go, my health had fallen off, and as we came home, I once again felt like a living dog of a man. On the day of Game 3, my tonsils swelled to the size of small plums. The infection that had plagued me in the season before returned and was spreading to my kidneys. Uremic convulsions — a hospital name for an unnameable pain — gave way to vascular ruptures, which gave way to intestinal cramps, which gave way to constriction of the abdominal cavity. The morning of Game 3 was the worst. I awoke to the sight of horrible black blotches, friggin' panoramas of mud, and I had to lie still for a few minutes until I could see clearly again. Inside, I was a bus wreck, and for the team, this did not look good.

I struggled that day not to let on that I was hurting so badly, but the fellas found out the hard way. We were wracked hard that night 5–2 by the surging Wings. By the third period, I couldn't stand in the crease without hanging over the crossbar for support. The young couple shouted jovially to me, "Look, Charlie, he bought me a ring!" but I could barely raise my arm to acknowledge them, let

alone sing or jibe or tell jokes. All game, Coach Gorman
was nervous and fidgety; he could sense the Red Wings
pulling the pendulum back in their favour. After the game,
one of our doctors forced a flashlight down my throat and
said my season was over. Gorman, looking grim as science,
took off his hat, wiped his forehead with the back of his
hand, leaned against the wall and said, "Go home and sleep
on it, Chuck."

"I haven't been able to sleep for three weeks. What
makes you think that tonight's going to be any different?"

"You need some rest."

"Just tell the fellas to get me one goal."

"What?"

"The next game. All I need is one goal."

Now, I haven't talked to the Big Fella yet, but I still
wonder whose design it was to have Game 4 go five periods — four hours — without a single goal. Was it some
muggins' idea of a joke? Because if it was, I hope they liked
the part where I nearly lost a lung hacking up blood into a
bucket between the third and fourth periods after taking
a puck in the throat. I hope they got a kick out of seeing a
dying man on his last legs throw his body teeth first into
a low-flying puck screaming in from the blueline, eating
Taffy Abel's skates on the way to the goalpost. I hope the
friggin' sadistic geeks up here enjoyed it when Abel's
300-pound bucket ass fell backward on me, booting my

consciousness halfway to Kalamazoo, Michigan. I feel vindictive for being toyed with by some Greater Being and his friggin' bridge-club cronies. I do. Yet I have no real regrets. I would not trade the day of April 10, 1934, for all the hair on young Wayne Gretzky's head.

It was a game to end all games, the papers said. We lasted five periods, me and Wilf Cude, the Wings goalie. He was a Welshman, I was a Scot, and we played stubbornly until neither of us could stand, until our bodies shut down and our instincts took over and drove us down the blind alleys of overtime. In periods three, four and five, we kicked out discs we didn't even know were coming. We made saves from our backsides staring up into the ceiling girders of Chicago Stadium. We stabbed pucks with our feet and deflected shots with the shafts of our goal sticks. We answered each other's saves, slowing and quickening the game's rhythm, freezing the puck at will, juggling it with our oversize mitts, kicking it into the corner, smothering it the way cats pounce on mice and dropping it stiff-armed behind the net like an apple falling out of a tree. From high atop the rafters of the new arena, Cude and I must have looked like two flightless acrobats in search of a trapeze. The crowd gasped through every kick and tuck, stretch and roll, their hands rushing to cover their eyes as the puck bounced and pogoed around the post or dipped and curved in its flight path toward the net.

In the mezzanines during intermission, fans were asking each other which goalie's magic would betray him first, and by the time we skated into overtime, it was anybody's guess. After three hours of hockey, our movement in front of the puck was like a strange dance by a dime-store magician trying to hypnotize a chicken. We looked stoned and silly out there. We were like B-grade actors playing ourselves, every move wild and exaggerated, a bijou performance of a lifetime.

Little Mush March finally won it in the fifth period to give Chicago its very first Stanley Cup. When the foghorn hollered to sound victory, I fell to my knees exhausted, the piss and sweat pouring out of me like rain as I looked across at the bench and saw the boys race toward me like loosed hounds. Six weeks later on a fine spring's day, the infection in my tonsils would take a death grip on my body and spread quickly to my brain, killing me easily in a brightly lit hospital in St. Boniface, Manitoba.

But in those last moments on the ice at Chicago Stadium and from where I sit now, watching Captain Ennui walk toward me, his hand in his sweater pocket, smoking a pipe, the checker board under his other arm, I wasn't thinking about how badly I felt at the game's end or how I could barely move or speak. No, I was thinking about poor Wilf Cude, sitting in the crease at the other end of the rink, his arms at his side like tired puppets, his face weary and sad. Red Wing players gathered around him, their arms draped over his sagging shoulders, their gloves patting his mussy head. For a minute, he stayed on his knees and so did I. His expression was as still as a bird's. In a few weeks, I would be dead at 30, but after all was said and done, I had won Game 4. Would Cude have traded places with me? I believe that he would have. Finally, he rose to his skates and glided off the ice. He disappeared down the runway like a canary into a dark tunnel.

To my left, there was quite a scene going on. A group of fans had run onto the ice and were drinking champagne and toasting the players and the crowd. The coaches and trainers were together in little groups, laughing and hugging one another. Taffy Abel lifted Mush March over his head with one arm, like Friar Tuck hoisting a banquet tray, and paraded him around the rink. Over in the corner, Conacher was shaking Artie Coulter's hand so hard I thought it would snap off. They were laughing and celebrating like little kids.

Out of nowhere, someone skated over and handed me the Stanley Cup. I saw my face in its reflection, and I looked all puffy and red-eyed and dazed. But I was smiling. So, like a real, bona fide, 100 per cent muggins, I sat there and cried a river. Hell, I cried buckets right there in front of thousands. Then Big Train Conacher saw me crying and soon the whole team was bawling their eyes out. The fans were shouting at me from their seats. They stamped their feet and cheered at the top of their lungs and rocked the building so hard that the boards were swaying like ocean waves. They threw rainbows of streamers and serpentines and flowers and hats onto the ice and they pretty well held the Stanley Cup parade right then and there in the rink. I heard the young couple behind me yell and scream and I recognized their voices. I stopped and I thought to myself, "Boy! They're getting married!" I looked back at them and yelled, "Congratulations!" and winked, hoisting the Cup high above my head. That was something. They kissed and exploded into confetti.

GARDINER, CHARLIE: Chicago — 1927–34

Regular Schedule

GP	W	L	T	MINS	GA	SO	AVG
316	112	152	52	19687	664	42	2.02

Playoff Schedule

GP	W	L	T	MINS	GA	SO	AVG	CUP WINS
21	12	6	3	1532	35	5	1.37	1

2

THE MONTREAL CANADIENS

BY WAYNE JOHNSTON

I DON'T LIVE IN MONTREAL ANY MORE, BUT "ROCKET" Richard still calls me every March 17 to talk about what happened to us on that day in 1955.

It begins even further back than that, really. In 1954, I was writing a satirical hockey column called The Gondola for the Montreal *Gazette* and NHL president Clarence Campbell was one of my favourite targets. He was forever calling my publisher, accusing me of bias, demanding that I be fired, threatening to sue. He said that I called him a dictator, though in fact it was the Rocket who had called him that.

The Rocket was "writing" a column, too. It was called *Le Tour du Chapeau* (Hat Trick) and appeared in a weekend paper called *Samedi-Dimanche*. "I can do your job in my spare time," the Rocket would say, teasing me and digging at me with his elbow, though actually it was I who was

Maurice Richard

doing his job in my spare time, for I was his ghostwriter.

Few people knew this until Campbell revealed it one day in one of the rival English papers. He said he was "unmasking" me, that francophones ought to know who was really writing Hat Trick, that it was not their beloved Rocket but an anglophone who was putting words in the Rocket's mouth.

Better to blame the hack than the hero, I suppose. If anything, I toned down the Rocket's opinions in a vain attempt to keep him out of trouble and I certainly never had to tell him what to say. He would phone me on Thursday nights and in a torrent of French give me the gist

of his column, often raving about some referee who in the last game had made a bad call, having been put up to it, he said, by Clarence Campbell. He said Campbell was doing the bidding of the other five owners, who knew that if they could "get" the Habs, they would make more money. This conspiracy theory, though it needed some fleshing out, was not as far-fetched as it sounds.

We got our chance to flesh it out in January 1954, when Campbell suspended Bernie "Boom Boom" Geoffrion for eight games because of a stick-swinging incident. The Rocket was incensed. "I'm not gonna play it safe this time," he said. "That bastard is out to get us and it's time someone said so." He, we, said so. Here are some excerpts from the installment of Hat Trick that did us in: "According to friends who watch President Campbell during games at the Forum, he smiles and openly shows pleasure when an opposing club scores against us…What did he do when Jean Béliveau was deliberately injured by Billy Mosienko of Chicago and Jack Evans of the Rangers? No penalty, no fine, no suspension…Let Campbell get busy with the other little goings-on…and not try to create publicity for himself at the expense of a good fellow like Boom Boom Geoffrion just because he is a French Canadian."

This time, we had played into Campbell's hands. As soon as I saw the column in print, I knew it. "He suckered us," the Rocket said. And he was right.

Campbell issued the Canadiens an ultimatum: get your house in order, or else. The next issue of *Samedi-Dimanche* announced the Rocket's "decision" to stick to hockey from now on and stop writing columns.

The following day a statement issued from league headquarters and said to have been written by the Rocket himself announced that he had "humbly and sincerely apologized to President Campbell and to the NHL governors for statements that I made in my column. I realize fully that the accusations made were unfounded and I am anxious that Mr. Campbell's integrity and honesty of the game be established beyond question…"

In The Gondola I wrote that I had resigned as Maurice Richard's ghostwriter and that the job was now being filled by Clarence Campbell. Campbell said this was libel and swore that, if he didn't get a retraction and an apology from me, he would sue. I told my editor that hell would freeze over first. Up to this point, he had been with me all the way where Campbell was concerned, but having seen what happened to the Rocket, he began to lose his nerve, wondering how far Campbell's reach might extend. He said he would write an "explanation" of my remarks that he thought would satisfy Campbell and append it in italics to the next installment of The Gondola.

The explanation included this sentence: "Mr. Fraser was not suggesting that Mr. Campbell actually decided what

Richard should say and wrote the apology himself, but only that, judging by the style, it was obvious that someone must have helped Richard with the wording of the statement, just as Mr. Fraser himself often helped Richard with the wording of his columns."

Campbell, in the rival paper, replied: "Is this how it's to be from now on? Mr. Fraser writes a column to which his editor must append an 'explanation'? This is a curious form of journalism indeed. I for one don't intend to spend my days decoding Mr. Fraser's columns. If he has something to say, he should come right out and say it."

The Editor's Explanation, which I abbreviated E.E., featured largely in my next column, though it was me and not the editor who wrote it. Having heard and apparently believed the somewhat embellished stories about my drinking habits, Campbell phoned me at home one night and called me a "Scotch-besotted son of a bitch" and my column "booze-inspired cant," and he wondered if I had ever written a word while I was sober or if there was anyone left alive who had ever seen me sober.

The next day in The Gondola I gave the following account of our conversation: "Mr. President called me on the phone yesterday. I made a suggestion. He made, and offered to help me carry out, a suggestion of his own. Said on the record I was off my rocker. Off the record, a good deal more. The words 'Scotch' and 'bitch' came up a lot.

(E.E.: Mr. Fraser and Mr. Campbell, though they rarely meet, chat frequently by phone, often sharing a chuckle over the unaccountable rumours that there exists between them some sort of animosity. The words 'Scotch' and 'bitch' came up frequently in their most recent conversation because Mr. Campbell had phoned Mr. Fraser to share with him the happy news that his terrier had just had a litter of puppies, three of whom were female. Mr. Fraser, who had been promised the pick of the litter and who has followed with much interest the course of Pokey's pregnancy these past few months, could not have been more pleased. As for the exchange of suggestions, it demonstrates perfectly the deep-seated mutual admiration that exists between these two and which no amount of professional rivalry can undermine.)"

The hyperearnest Campbell seemed more bewildered than anything else. "Is this journalism?" he asked in the rival paper. "Is there another paper in the world that would print such drivel?"

A few days after his farewell column appeared, the Rocket and I met for a drink to talk about what had happened.

"I still got hockey," he said.

"And I still have The Gondola," I said.

"You still got it for now," the Rocket said. "You better watch yourself with that bastard."

When I described to him one of Campbell's apoplectic phone calls, he said, laughing and shaking his head, "You sure know how to get his goat." Then, abruptly, he stopped laughing, as if some grievance he had momentarily forgotten had come back to him, the smile fading awkwardly from his face.

He looked away from me as though he were staring into a fire. "I don't know what the hell everybody wants from me," he said. "Nothing I do is good enough for them. Fifty goals in 50 games — I got all five goals in one game, they gave me all three stars, and people complained that I never passed the puck."

Only on the ice was he able to rid himself of this aggrieved self-consciousness and it seemed to me that, for him, this was the point of playing hockey, to forget himself completely, immerse himself totally in a world in which merit, strength, talent and courage could prevail, a world in which to have been well born or have important parents or influential friends was of no advantage whatsoever.

"You get Campbell's goat, too, you know," I said. "Every time you score a goal, you get his goat." He shook his head almost imperceptibly and rolled his glass of beer between his hands.

Though the Rocket normally had a short fuse, the explosion this time was delayed, so delayed, in fact, that the press in other cities talked about the Rocket having at last been defused by Campbell. "This Rocket is a dud," said one New York writer who usually criticized the Rocket for being too hot-tempered. It was not until more than a year later, on March 13, 1955, in a game against the Bruins at the Boston Garden, that the inevitable explosion came.

The Rocket was really flying that day. It was as though the instant he crossed the blueline, he recognized the Bruin goalie, "Sugar" Jim Henry, as some mortal enemy of his whom he hadn't seen in years and to whom he might never get this close again. Even from the distance of the press box, you could see the sudden change in his eyes, as if some fever, some delirium had just kicked in. It was as if it was only to hide his real intentions that he even bothered with the puck, as if this whole hockey thing was just some ruse that allowed him to pursue with impunity his real vocation, which was making goalies like Henry suffer. But though Richard faced him all alone half a dozen times, he couldn't put the puck past him. And each time Henry made a save, the Rocket became that much more upset, once crashing into him on purpose, knocking the net off its moorings.

"Maurice doesn't like goalies," said his brother Henri, who was sitting beside me in the press box that night. He spoke with an air of sombre, almost grave confidentiality as if to say that if you want to understand the Rocket, therein lies the key.

I looked at Jim Henry, the Goalie. He was everything Richard was not and nothing that he wished to be. Passive, static, cumbersome, uniquely attired, barely able to skate, arbitrarily endowed with special powers and exemptions, waiting for the puck to come to him, hoping against hope that it wouldn't, pouncing on it when it did and thereby bringing to a standstill the furious frenzy of the game — how *could* the Rocket like the Goalie?

"I think he likes the officials even less," I said, as Elmer Lach and Hector "Toe" Blake tried to keep the Rocket from getting at the referee, Frank Udvari, who had given him a penalty for interfering with Jim Henry. Henri laughed. Lach and Blake all but carried the Rocket to the box; once inside, he refused to sit down and continued glaring at Udvari.

For the Rocket, the referee was a limiting, frustrating force, an agency of opposition, a "Thwart," as I called him in my column, always imagining a kind of gravid, toad-like creature. The Rocket, every time he cut toward the net, dark eyes flashing, was out to get the Thwart, the one flaw in his ice paradise. In life, the Thwart appeared in many guises, on the ice in only three: goalie, linesman, referee.

The Canadiens, who badly needed a win if they hoped to finish first overall, were losing 4–2 at the 14-minute mark of the third period and the Rocket's frustration was at its peak when what Campbell would call the "incident" occurred.

Boston defenceman Hal Laycoe high-sticked the Rocket as he made his umpteenth attack on Henry, cutting him badly on the forehead. The Rocket was dazed, though not so dazed that he couldn't hear Laycoe say, "This frog is really a chicken." In the melee that followed, Richard broke his stick across Laycoe's back, did likewise with sticks he wrestled away from several other players, and when linesman Cliff Thompson tried to intervene, he unambiguously punched him twice in the face. Whether, with blood-blurred vision, the Rocket knew it was Thompson he was punching is anybody's guess. He told me afterward he didn't, but there were things the Rocket would never own up to, not even to a friend.

Three days later, on March 16, the Rocket appeared in front of Campbell at league headquarters in Montreal. It was a classic case of worlds colliding. I was not there, of course, but the Rocket told me about it and I have often pictured it. On one side of the desk, I see the son of a Gaspé machinist; himself a machinist by training; a mythically talented hockey player who is living out his lifelong dream of playing for the Montreal Canadiens; an authority-defying, discipline-abhorring temperamental renegade; a Catholic; a francophone. On the other side of the desk, his desk in his office on his floor of the Sun Life building, towering symbol of English-dominated Montreal, I see an Oxford-educated lawyer, a Rhodes scholar, a failed hockey player, a one-time referee, a former Nuremberg prosecutor, an authoritarian, a disciplinarian, a Protestant anglophone, the very epitome of urbane rectitude and propriety: in short, a Thwart. They are so unalike, so opposite, I cannot imagine them speaking to each other.

After his meeting with Campbell, before the suspension had even been announced, the Rocket phoned me at my office. "I'm out for the rest of the season," he said. "Playoffs too. Everything." I was dumbstruck. It was so far in excess of what I had expected that I could not believe it. It seemed Campbell had abandoned even the pretense of evenhandedness. I told the Rocket, not believing it myself, that Campbell was just trying to make a point, that he would wait a while and then reinstate him for the playoffs.

"No he won't," the Rocket said, in a tone I had never heard him use before. "They got me this time," he said, on the verge of tears. "They finally got me. The Art Ross is gone. I'll never win it now. This was my one chance. I'll never get this close again."

Though he had many times led the league in goals, he had never managed enough assists to win a scoring championship. It was his belief that official scorers in other cities withheld assists from him and gave "soft," undeserved assists to his rivals to make sure he didn't win.

This year, he was, with three games to go in the regular season, leading the scoring race by several points. In second place, and the only real threat to overtake him, was his own teammate, Boom Boom Geoffrion. "You'll win the

Art Ross," I said, as if I was taking revenge for him by saying so. "Boomer will let you win."

The next morning, The Gondola began this way: "The number of Joseph Stalin's enemies who are still drawing breath and the number of Clarence Campbell's who are still drawing paycheques is about the same. (E.E.: Mr. Fraser is not directly comparing Mr. Campbell to Joseph Stalin who has murdered 25 million of his countrymen just to keep himself in power, an act of which Mr. Campbell is obviously incapable, since his countrymen number only 20 million. Rather, the foregoing is a simile in which irony is — we hope you will agree — wittily employed to make a point. Let me say, for one too modest to do so on his own behalf, how clever.)"

On any other day, that column might have got me fired. But on March 17, St. Patrick's Day, 1955, most people were so preoccupied, they didn't notice it. By midmorning, the Richard suspension was common knowledge, and the city of Montreal and the province of Quebec were in a frenzy. In the newsroom, we listened to the radio stations, both French and English, hardly able to believe what we heard. Callers to phone-in shows who sounded as though they meant business swore they would kill Campbell before the day was out; one man said the Sun Life building would be blown up if Campbell did not relent by six o'clock and reinstate Richard; another vowed that if Campbell showed up for tonight's game between the Habs and the Red Wings, he would be carried from the Forum in a box. Most callers lapsed so quickly into venomous obscenity, they had to be cut off.

Word went out that, though the Montreal police and City Hall advised Campbell, for his own and everybody else's sake, to stay away from the Forum, he had told them he would not be bullied and would be in his accustomed seat at game time. When I arrived at 7:30 p.m., the Forum was surrounded by a mob of thousands. One man held aloft a stick from which hung an effigy of Campbell with a noose around its neck, head tilted sideways, tongue sticking out. So good a likeness was it, with its black suit and rakishly tilted black hat, that people were screaming and shaking their fists at it.

In the press box, and in the stands before the opening faceoff, the one topic of conversation was whether Campbell would show up for the game or not. His two seats were at the St. Catherine Street end of the Forum, directly behind and above the goal, and by the time of the opening faceoff, they were still empty. "He won't show," I heard someone say.

But show he did, fashionably late, his entrance seemingly timed so as to be witnessed by as many people as possible, about halfway through the first period, accompanied by his fiancée, Phyllis, as though this were just another game.

There they were, the president and his soon-to-be first lady, escorted by a single usher, though 150 uniformed police officers were conspicuously present in the building; there he was, the dapper villain, in his pin-striped black suit and trademark wide-brimmed black hat; and there she was, following trustingly, faithfully behind him in her pink coat, on her head what might have been an Easter bonnet, festively adorned with flowers, her white purse on her arm. Apparently oblivious to what she had let herself in for, she was smiling, looking cheerfully bemused by the uproar of boos and catcalls that greeted their arrival. ("What are we doing tonight, Clarence darling?" "Oh, I thought we'd have dinner and then go start a riot at the Forum." "A riot? What should I wear?" "Something provocative, my dear.")

Up and down the press box, it was generally agreed the

man was crazy just to show up himself, but to drag poor Phyllis into it — well what was one to make of it? I have often tried to imagine him explaining it to the satisfaction of her parents.

The enigmatic Phyllis. For those who theorize that Campbell knew or even hoped that his presence at the game would start a riot, she is the catch, for surely he would not knowingly have risked her safety, and if you give him that much credit, you are left with this: he must really have believed that he could face down the mob, that they wouldn't dare do what the rest of us had not the slightest doubt that they would do. But could anybody, even Clarence Campbell, be that blind?

It seemed that, even when the fans began making good on their threats, he could not or simply would not believe it. When people started throwing things at them, he sat there, affecting a kind of stoic obliviousness to the fact that people were pelting his fiancée with rotten eggs, that hot dogs, hamburgers, French fries and Cokes were raining down on them from every quarter. They sat there, the two of them, not even going so far toward acknowledging what was happening as to shield themselves, apparently trusting their respective hats to do the job. People in the immediate vicinity got out of the line of fire, leaving them isolated, the bull's-eye in the middle of a circle of vacated seats.

Still they sat there, beneath what soon became a deluge

of debris: Phyllis with her purse on her lap, looking as though she was calling upon her last reserves of poise, and her betrothed, perhaps only now beginning to realize the extent of his miscalculation and hoping against hope that some sort of face-saving resolution to their predicament might still be possible, grimly intent on the game. I couldn't help feeling sorry for them, however much they had brought it on themselves, nor could I resist feeling a kind of perverse admiration for this display of Waspish stoic pluck. I hoped that, for their own sakes, they would soon leave or be convinced to leave.

On the ice, the game continued, though the Canadiens were so distracted and incensed by the arrival of Campbell that they gave up three quick goals and were soon losing 4–1, which did nothing to improve the mood of the crowd.

It was at this point that I saw the Rocket. I'd known he was in the building, but I'd assumed that he was somewhere in the area behind the Canadiens bench. In fact, he was not more than 50 feet from Campbell, directly below him in the area behind the St. Catherine goal, sitting by himself on a folding chair.

From where he sat, he could see Campbell and Phyllis, but they seemed to have either not noticed or to be ignoring him. It is a sight I will never forget: Richard all by himself on that folding chair, looking so out of place, so out of his element, Richard in his street clothes, grounded, mere shoes on his feet instead of skates, craning his neck to see the action on the ice, which might as well have been a million miles away. Every now and then he turned around to look at Campbell, whose predicament he seemed at first to be enjoying. As time went on, however, and the barrage showed no signs of letting up, he began to look nervous, casting quick glances over his shoulder at Campbell and his fiancée and around him at the mob, who were reaching out toward him with their hands, supplicant, clamouring, as if they were waiting to hear what he wanted them to do, as if, at one word or sign from him, they were prepared to do anything.

It must have dawned on him that his sitting there in full view of the mob was only making matters worse. Taking one last look at Campbell, he grabbed his chair and ran off down the tunnel. "There goes the Rocket," someone in the press box said.

Even when the first period ended, Campbell and his fiancée refused to leave their seats. They were surrounded now by a ring of security and police officers who were obviously pleading with them to go before it was too late. The cops looked terrified and helpless, dodging debris as best they could, looking behind them and at one another. Clearly, although they had predicted trouble, they were not prepared for anything like this nor, judging by their faces, had they ever seen its like before.

Still, Campbell and Phyllis sat on through it, sat there,

up to their knees in paper cups, eggs, bottles, boxes, hot dogs, fruit, tomatoes, hats, programs, newspapers, over-shoes. The barrage was, if anything, increasing.

Phyllis took hold of Campbell's arm in both hands and, turning toward him, pressed her face against his shoulder as though to cuddle into him, as though she had felt a sudden rush of affection for him. It was such a pathetic gesture and the first acknowledgement from either of them that anything was wrong. "Why don't they make a break for it, for God's sake?" I said. "They're just sitting there. Doesn't he care what happens to her? Look at him." I wondered if they might simply be too scared to move, to turn around and face for as long as it would take to reach the exits the screaming mob behind them. We were all getting nervous and I think those of us whose papers had that day printed pieces critical of Campbell even felt a little guilty. I know I did. The whole press row was on its feet. We were shouting our exasperation with security who, we thought, should have stopped standing on ceremony and simply carried them out for their own good. But perhaps, even amid all that chaos, even faced with the virtual certainty that, if they didn't move them soon, it would be too late, it was simply unthinkable to the cops to lay hands on the man or prevail against his wishes.

Even people in parts of the Forum far distant from where Campbell sat were screaming at them now and throwing things in their direction that had no hope of reaching them. Sixteen thousand people were on their feet and facing the St. Catherine end of the rink, shaking their fists and chanting with a kind of revolutionary fervour, "*On veut Richard. À bas Campbell*" (We want Richard. Down with Campbell), as if they were staging a coup by which Campbell would be overthrown and Richard would take his place.

A young fellow in a black leather jacket came running over from the adjacent section, ducked under the linked arms of the cops and, incredibly, unthinkably, began pummelling Campbell with both fists, standing in front of him and teeing off while Campbell covered up as best he could, crossing his arms before his face. That famous black, somehow infuriating hat of his went flying from his head, at which there went up throughout the Forum a great roar of approval. It was an almost surreally unlikely sight, the untouchable, unassailable, insulated Campbell being roughed up by this hooligan, this infiltrator from a world whose very existence Campbell was barely willing to acknowledge and only then to hold it in contempt. Throughout the beating, which couldn't have lasted more than a few seconds, though it seemed to go on forever, Phyllis kept clinging to Campbell's arm, hindering his efforts to defend himself, her purse flailing on her arm as he pulled her about this way and that.

By the time the cops pulled Black Jacket off, he had landed several blows. Campbell, looking dazed, dabbed at his mouth with the back of his hand to see if it was bleeding. As two cops stood on either side of him, hands solicitously on his shoulders, another leaned close to him and said something, at which Campbell vigorously shook his head. He began rearranging his clothing and Phyllis reached behind and, just as a woman was about to snatch it up, grabbed his hat and replaced it on his head to a great chorus of boos from the Forum fans.

I think it occurred to Campbell, as it did to me, that that might be it, that he had weathered the worst and, as he was still sitting there, he had won and they had lost. I still think to this day that, with the assault on Campbell, things had reached a kind of climax that would ultimately have had on the fans a sobering, even shame-inducing effect.

It was then, however, one section away from Campbell, that the bomb some say was meant for him went off, a smoke bomb we thought at first until we noticed how frantically people fled from it, at which point we knew it must be tear gas. Directly below us, people began coughing, weeping, gasping for breath, holding their throats as if they were choking.

At last, at the arrival at their seats of Montreal police chief Leggett, Campbell and Phyllis got up and followed him and his escort of a dozen cops toward the exit. The last

I saw of them, Campbell was holding a handkerchief to his mouth with one hand and had his free arm around Phyllis, who had pulled her coat up around her head, her shoulders convulsing as she coughed from the effects of the tear gas. They could claim a victory of sorts, I suppose, though the price of it would soon become apparent.

An usher came running in to tell us that the fire chief, because of the possibility of mass panic, had ordered the Forum evacuated, which meant the by now all-but-forgotten game had been forfeited to the Red Wings. The tear gas had drifted up to the press box by this time and I was feeling its effects. It felt as though the skin were being seared from the inside of my throat; I was coughing painfully; tears were streaming down my face.

The press box emptied out and some of us, to avoid the panic at the exits, holed up in a washroom, coughing, sputtering, loosening ties, leaning against the wall and sliding down to the floor, which we could feel shaking beneath us. We had to shout to make ourselves heard, so loud was the roar from outside. It sounded, at one point, as though the Forum were falling down and I remember wondering how much longer it could hold.

When finally the roar subsided and the shaking stopped, we opened the washroom door and, as you might after a tornado has passed over, peeked out to assess the damage. We were about to head downstairs when we met a firefighter coming up who told us we'd better not try to leave as there was a full-scale riot going on outside the Forum, the glass front of which was all but gone.

The tear gas had drifted up into the rafters by this time and dispersed, so the air was breathable again. I went back up to the press box with a couple of other reporters, intending to wait out the riot.

We'd been there almost an hour when my phone rang. It was Canadiens general manager Frank Selke, who told me he had the Rocket in his office and was trying to convince him to address the mob by bullhorn from the ladder of a fire truck. "Maybe they'll listen to him," Selke said. "There won't be a Forum much longer if somebody doesn't do something." He said the Rocket had heard that I was still in the building and wanted to speak to me before making up his mind.

An usher escorted me to Selke's office, the door of which was open. Selke and Canadiens owner Senator Donat Raymond were sitting silently in the outer room, on opposite sides of a secretary's desk, nervously smoking cigarettes, their hats on their laps. They stood up when I walked in as people anxious about a sick relative might do at the sight of a doctor. "He's in there," Selke said, motioning toward the door of the inner office, which was closed.

I went in and there was the Rocket, sitting by himself on a leather couch, leaning forward, his forearms resting on his legs, hands clasped, head bowed. He looked up at me. "There's a full-scale riot going on out there," he said, as if he couldn't believe it had anything to do with him. "Selke's afraid they might burn down the Forum. They're tearing St. Catherine Street to pieces. Cars are on fire. Stores are on fire. They're stealing everything in sight. People might get killed because of me."

"Not because of you," I said. "It's not your fault. It's that fool Campbell's fault, if it's anybody's."

"Selke said . . ."

"Never mind what Selke said. You don't have to do anything you don't want to do."

"What do you think?" he said. The question, I saw by the way he looked at me, was not so much "Should I do it?" as "Can I do it, what should I say, will they listen to me, what if they don't?" He had never, in all the time I'd known him, worn such a look of dread. His demons — self-consciousness, self-doubt and fear of failure — for so long unreckoned with, were rising up against him all at once. Selke had no idea what he was asking him to do. I imagined it, the Rocket alone atop the ladder, holding a bullhorn, the taciturn, word-clumsy, diffident Rocket trying to quell with words a riot he had started with his hands. Between being, for a mob in such a frenzy, the object of worship and the object of vilification, there might not be much to choose. Images of him being carried off to God knows where to God knows what end kept running through my mind. I thought of Dionysius whose followers so loved him that they tore him limb from limb.

"Don't do it," I said. "It won't work anyway. Don't do it." I said the sight of him would only work up the crowd to an even greater pitch and that, instead of dispersing, they would likely carry him down St. Catherine on their shoulders. He hung his head as if we both knew I was only saying what he wanted me to say, as if he was ashamed for needing me to say it. He put his face in his hands and cried, his shoulders shaking.

We left the Forum, the Rocket and I, in Senator Raymond's white chauffeur-driven limousine. Because several streets were blocked by overturned and burning cars, we had to drive along St. Catherine for a while to find an exit. And there was nothing one could do that was more obviously, more flagrantly not in the spirit of the riot than to drive a car. We saw the windows of other cars smashed in, their occupants ducking for cover. The windows of the limousine, aside from being tinted so that no one could see inside, were reinforced. From inside, the sounds of the riot were strangely muted, the limousine moving through what might have been another element, so remote from ours did it seem. I tried to resist the illusion this encouraged that we were safe, inaccessible. I needn't have bothered for, as we were pelted with rocks and bricks, little webs began appearing in the glass.

"You better get us out of here," I had no sooner told the driver than we were forced by rioters standing in the street to stop. They crowded round and pressed their faces flat against the rear side windows as though looking in. It was hard to believe they couldn't see us. They made faces, stuck out their tongues, spit, banged on the windows with their fists, one guy hammering at mine with a woman's high-heel shoe. For a time that would often come back to me in dreams, we were hemmed in by their faces, peering sightlessly at us, at their beloved Rocket who would never again, when he played, be able to forget that they were watching. Finally, something else caught their interest and as they ran off, we sped away.

For two miles, like some undeviating whirlwind, the riot had roared up St. Catherine, from Atwater to University, where, with loot from the stores, the rioters had built a barricade. We saw only four blocks' worth, but even along that short stretch, it was impossible to take it all in. Certain seemingly discrete images linger in my mind: a team of rioters overturning a car, rhythmically rocking it until they got one set of wheels off the ground, then flipping it upside down, the car, because of its convex roof, rotating slowly on the pavement, the rioters standing round it in a circle, pushing it to make it spin; a lone cop surrounded by looters, looking around for help that wasn't there; a newspaper kiosk completely enclosed in flame; a stretch of sidewalk littered surreally with television sets, their screens smashed in; one intersection, like the ice after a player's third goal of the game, strewn with hats of every description from some gutted milliner's shop; rioters running from a delicatessen with oversize glass bottles crammed with pickles held high above their heads and hurling them at cars.

At last we turned off onto a side street and soon were out of earshot of the riot, passing houses that were mostly dark though in the downstairs window of one a little boy waved as the limousine went by.

The next day, the Rocket faced his demons after all. At 7:15 p.m., he went on television and radio and read the statement that I had written for him, the last bit of ghost-writing I ever did on his behalf.

He spoke from the Canadiens dressing room, in front of a mass of microphones, first in French and then in English, his Number 9 sweater hanging on the wall behind him. "I will take my punishment," the Rocket said. "I will come back next year to help the club and to help the younger players win the Cup." There was no more rioting in Montreal.

Those who knew him and heard him speak that day said there was something in his voice they had never heard before. Humility, one writer said, but that was not quite it. He spoke in the tone of a young man who can see in the distance a point he will never get past, the limit of a leash that, until then, he hadn't even known that he was wearing.

They said he was never again, after 1955, the player that he used to be. They talked about his spirit having been broken, about him having lost his nerve. There were some who said that, even off the ice, he was never the same, and I who have known him for nearly 50 years must admit that this is true.

But here is something else that they should know: on a grey day in 1984, at the funeral of Clarence Campbell, at his graveside, in fact, when we were asked by some reporter if time had changed our minds about the man and I mumbled something about Campbell having an undisputed place in hockey history, the Rocket shook his head. "He was wrong," he said, walking away. "If they ask me on my deathbed, I will tell them he was wrong."

The last hockey game at the Montreal Forum took place on March 11, 1996. All of the living Canadien captains passed a ceremonial torch from hand to hand; the oldest of these, the first torchbearer, was Maurice "Rocket" Richard. — Ed.

3

THE DETROIT RED WINGS

BY JUDITH FITZGERALD

Saturday Evenings in the
Church of Hockey Night in Canada

WHEN YOU GROW UP WITH GUYS LIKE GORDIE HOWE AND Grandpa, you grow up street smart, turf tough and ever rough and ready. Long before you learn the alphabet, you learn the way things are, the way things went and the way they'll always be. And, if you get lucky, you never forget 'em.

Several decades after the facts, I vividly remember every detail of that catastrophic 1950 night when a case of bad timing nearly cost Howe his life. I remember the dribbly-grey day, the wind-blistery night, the violent smear of brilliant crimson clotting beneath my hero's skull as he lay obliterated amid pop-glittering flashes of photographers'

Gordie Howe

bulbs. I shall never forget those faces frozen with fear, that premonitory hush, the collective howl of horror and heart-break when Howe's buddies delicately removed my hero's lifeless form from that sea of blood and ice.

So even though I wasn't even *old* enough to go to Detroit's Olympia with Grandpa that fateful March night, I remember like yesterday the events he relished and embellished each and every time "ol' stinky Blinky" got into his famous fisticuffs and fights.

Grandpa, one scrappy Québécois named Gabby, migrated to Toronto in the latter half of the 1940s, right around the time "ol' stinky Blinky" joined the Red Wings. Looking back, I suspect the die-hard Leaf man secretly worshipped Gordie Howe, my one and only idol; however, his fever-pitched vocal eruptions will most likely remain imprinted on my brain forever: "Tsk-tsk and *tabernac!* My grand-daughter's gone off the deep end, for sure, for sure! Blinky? That stinky Detroit Red Wing nut case?"

Eyes glazing, arms flapping, fingers jabbing and colour rising high crimson in the gaunt hollows of his wrinkle-creased face, Grandpa glares and fumes with fulsome delight whenever I mention the player he loves to hate, belittle and endlessly berate. *Hell's bells and sacrifice!*

"*Merde, merde, merde,*" he moans in my direction, mock-maudlin features telegraphing deathly disgust, "wait 'til you grow up! *Then!* Then, you'll learn *the truth* about your precious darling Blinky!"

This morning — *the truth* uppermost in mind — various hockey books, bibles and microfilm copies of 1950s *Telegram* sports fronts collapse intervening decades and several living snapshots fan out on the floor of my brain: I taste sour metallic IPA bottle caps and smell the woody aroma of Black Cat tobacco, Grandpa meting out precise amounts of loose grains, delicate paper creased open by nicotine-stained fingers one moment, rolling off the tip of his tongue the next, measured *tamp, tamp, tamp* on the rose-flecked oilcloth covering the table completing the ritual.

Our kitchen resembles a poor man's Hockey Hall of Fame — huge team calendars, Leaf captain Ted Kennedy's autograph on a broken CCM stick, my younger brother Bobby's tabletop hockey game, programs, plus the usual paraphernalia fanatics inevitably accumulate.

Grandpa tacks sport-section fronts from the Toronto *Tely* on the wall above the kitchen table, strategically enshrining eye-level black-and-pink photographs of Teeder Kennedy sprawling into goalie

Turk Broda, Detroit's Black Jack Stewart helping teammate Sid Abel carry an unconscious Howe on a stretcher and the Toronto captain's bewildered and sheepish mug (so I'd confront *the truth* at least three times a day).

The truth — always a murky issue when viewed through time's window — may never see the light. As both Grandpa and NHL president Clarence Campbell saw *the* incident that would eventually assume mythic importance in both the lore of the game and Howe's enduring fame, my idol's death-defying collision with the boards at the Olympia could not be pinned on Kennedy. No way. No how. Nosirree.

The truth? Four years after Howe broke into the major-league ranks with the Wings, he'd not only galvanized the game with his philosophy of "religious — *It is better to give than receive* — hockey," he'd also proved his prowess as a recklessly crazy maniac who could outshoot, outscore, outmanoeuvre and outsmart any player foolish enough to dally with the driving force of the Production Line.

As Maple Leafster Eddie Shack recalls (in *Squads and Demigods*), Howe regularly effected "pacts of non-aggression" with overzealous players; likewise, Howe himself points out he learned early such agreements helped avoid injury and ensured a long career. When a player did attack him, he would invariably get the last hit, even if it meant playing under "retributive-strike" conditions for five or six games.

By March 28, 1950, Howe's do-or-die reputation, well known among players unlucky enough to tangle with the titan, would certainly have figured in Kennedy's treatment of — and respect for — the agile ambidextrist.

"We were playing the Maple Leafs in Detroit," recalls Howe (in *Years of Glory*). "I was chasing Teeder Kennedy. He was coming down the left side of the rink, to my right, and I was going to run him into the boards. But my first thought was to intercept the pass I figured he'd make to Sid Smith, who was coming down the centre of the ice. I glanced back at Smith and put my stick down where I thought the pass might be going.

"What I didn't know as I turned back toward Kennedy was that, in the instant I'd turned away, he'd let the pass go, and now he was bringing up his stick to protect himself from my hitting him. I was still low, and the blade of the stick caught me in the face — tore my right eyeball, broke my nose and cheekbone. As if this wasn't bad enough, I then smashed into the boards, giving myself a whale of a concussion.

"They took me to the hospital in an ambulance, and within minutes I was on the operating table and they were drilling a hole in the side of my skull to relieve the pressure. I was awake through all this; I could hear the drill against the bone. But what was really on my mind was that they'd shaved part of my head. I was at an age when I needed my hair, and I was thinking, 'Oh, gosh, no, what am I going to look like?'"

When Red Wing officials flew in Howe's mother and sister from Saskatoon, Saskatchewan, Motown shut down. The hustle-bustle of the gritty industrial city ground to a halt, prepared for the jolt and prayed it wouldn't happen.

"For a couple of days, nobody let me sleep," says Howe. "They were afraid I'd go into a coma and never come out. They'd come along and scrape the bottoms of my feet every few minutes and say, 'Don't go to sleep on us.'"

He didn't; instead, the resurrected Mr. Miracle attended the final game of the 1949–50 season and went weak in the knees when his Wings beat the New York Rangers 4–3 to claim the Stanley Cup: "My injury had been a big story in the papers and, as the Cup was being presented, the crowd started calling for me; I'd been watching from a seat near the bench. But as I went out on the ice, my worst fear came to pass. Someone grabbed my hat, and there I was in front of 16,000 fans with a big bald patch on my head. Oh, it was awful!"

As awful as Howe considered that crowning moment, less than a month after his near-death experience, his huge hands clasped hockey's Holy Grail for the first time while 16,000 fans simply went joyously berserk or, as Grandpa preferred, "Them Yankees flipped their lids."

☆

The truth? I shall never forget Grandpa's version of Blinky and Teeder Bear's tête-à-tête, especially because his repeated retellings always included quasi-mythic tragicomic elements:

Kennedy elicits near-tear histrionics complete with chequered hankie while Howe's "Blinky" nickname — freshly minted in the dawning era of eye-irritating television klieg lights and done to death by Grandpa — induces a string of damnatory epithets that leap from burning lips and run for cover in sheer sneer fear.

Now, according to Grandpa, Teeder truthfully told the *Tely* he saw Howe coming at him, stepped out of the way and stood powerless as he watched Number 9 crash into the boards. And, again according to Grandpa, Kennedy swore he'd take an oath to the effect his stick never touched Howe; further, Teeder Bear couldn't and wouldn't inflict that kind of injury on anyone, let alone Howe, a player already well known for his rough-and-rowdy attitude on ice.

"I was there! I saw the whole thing with my own two eyes! Here's Teeder minding his own beeswax skating with the puck…Then, what? That crafty Blinky sneaks up on him and is gonna cream him but…Teeder just puts on the brakes. Blinky takes a bite out of the boards! Slams them face first! That slinky Blinky, that Wing Nut! Look it! They didn't even call a penalty? What does *that* tell you?"

"*The truth,* right?"

"Right, Bobby, right. Teeder Bear innocent. Howe guilty. Case closed."

"But, Grandpa, Wings won the Cup, right?"

"*Câlisse!* They did so, *and* not a Blinky in sight! Oh, that Howe. He's one of the slickest, smoothest, smartest, sneakiest sons-of-bitches ever to lace up a pair of skates. Look it here! It says it all."

"Read it, Grandpa, what does it say?"

"It says, 'Teeder innocent. Howe guilty. Case closed.'"

"Where, Grandpa, where? Show me!"

"Right here, see? Right above the picture. 'Young Gordie Howe busts his head on the boards 'cause of his own stupid fault and Teeder didn't do nothing wrong.'"

Grandpa reads the headlines, captions and stories to us from the sports sections he religiously tacks to that wall. Usually, he reads them between periods, turning down the volume on the cream-coloured Bakelite radio so we don't miss his points: "Look it here," he jabs, "plain as the nose on your face: Howe intended to knock Teeder Bear's block off but the captain plain outsmarted the dumb right winger. See? Look at this picture! I was there! I saw it all with my own two eyes. Your guy made the big mistake and almost killed hisself! Blood, blood, buckets of blood and ol' Blinky in Cuckoo Land! *Stoo-oo-pid!*"

"But, he's okay now, Grandpa, and smart!"

"You think so? Look at this picture. Does this look like a smart guy, Bobby?"

"Nope."

"See? There you go. Look at this proof: 'Gordon Howe, the best right winger in the NHL *after* the Rocket, is just a dumb-dumb.' Now you believe me? It's right here in the *Tely*."

"Read it to me, Grandpa, read it!"

"See? Here? Right under the dumb-dumb's picture."

Of course, I couldn't read it.

Saturday nights, my mother — who considered hockey for the birds — would borrow $2 for what Grandpa called "her stupid love-stuffy movie." He'd remind her to think of our good name when she traipsed down Yonge Street to the Rio.

After she'd depart, Grandpa always asked the same question: "She go?"

"She go."

"Good. Get the beer, eh, Doré?"

"Yes, Grandpa." I retrieve the case of IPA from the trunk of the battered blue Buick; Grandpa lines up his freshly rolled supply of cigs in the Black Cat tin; then, we get down to business.

"Doré, Blinky suits up for them Red Things. There'll be a hot time in the old town tonight. Now, who's the best team d'hockey?"

"*Wings,* Grandpa, not *Things.* Wings!"

"Bobby?"

"Leafs," he snickers, "right? Things! *Sacrifice!*"

Grandpa glares at Bobby.

Bobby studies the flowers on the linoleum, little pink roses adorning perfect crisscrossing rows of ivy.

"*Sacrifice!*" growls Grandpa, "you don't talk such words, Robert."

When Grandpa says Bobby's real name, Bobby sounds like a robber.

"I'm sorry, Grandpa. I just mean the Leafs are gooder than her team."

"Not gooder," I correct, "*better…*"

"Right," concurs Grandpa, "Leafs *is* better! Leafs is the best!"

"The berry best," adds Bobby, "and Doré's a dumb-dumb."

"And you're a boobie."

"By the jumpin'," scowls Grandpa, "enough! Just get your Grandpa a bottle o' beer, eh?"

☆

Naturally, during our ritual pregame wieners-and-beans confabs, we flank Grandpa who presides over the proceedings with all the pomposity and pontificating punch he can muster after working the janitorial beat at the bank downtown on Belinda Street.

Grandpa invariably begins our discussions with homespun lessons about the evils lurking on Yonge Street: "*Bien,* guys, she's probably at some tavern by now…"

"Mom went to the movies, Grandpa."

"*Phlitz!* She just says that for your benefit. She went to the nightclub for sure."

We don't know the difference between dayclubs and nightclubs, so we simply agree with Grandpa.

Neither Bobby nor I ever understood how anybody could skip our family congregations in the Church of Hockey Night in Canada, especially during *these* playoffs, particularly with Grandpa galumphing in his gloats ever since "ol' stinky Blinky" made his "stupidest move yet" and nearly met his Maker.

Grandpa does the incident to death each time Motown rumbles into the Gardens and inappropriately flattens his Leafs; however, by March he turns his attention to more pressing matters, namely the Leafs' valiant struggle to topple my Cup-defending Wings during the down-to-the-wire race for the regular-season crown.

He whoops and hollers when Leafs set new win and point records; he dismisses Detroit's first-place record-setting finish by belittling the team's Rookie of the Year, freshly acquired goaltender Terry Sawchuk.

"Yeah," he scoffs, "the dumb Things trade Harry Lumley, the goalie who won them the Cup, and they trade away Stewart and Pete Babando for a bunch of babies. Smart cookies. They think Bob Goldham and Metro Prystai gonna win Stanley? Over my Leafs' dead bodies."

"They've got the best goalie in the whole NHL, Grandpa! They've got Marcel Pronovost, and don't forget Red Kelly and the Production Line…"

"The *what?*"

"The Production Line: Gordie Howe, Ted Lindsay and Sid Abel!"

"Lemme see…the Blinky Line? *Those* guys? Ain't they dead yet?"

"Grandpa! They set new records! Gordie scored 43 goals and got 43 assists! That's the best! You know it!"

"I don't know that. *Aujourd'hui roi, demain rien.* The team that wins the Cup's the best. I only know *that.* We'll see…"

☆

And see we did. We sat, we listened and we cast our eyes on page after humiliating page following each humiliating defeat, defeats made all the more humbling because Grandpa indubitably seized every available opportunity to reinforce his convictions concerning Howe's infelicitous mortal sin against the virtuous Kennedy.

"*Merde, merde, merde,*" he'd splutter and spume, his abiding sense of rightness inevitably interfering with his almost insufferable self-righteousness: "Blinky just gots what he's always deserved! An eye for an eye! A tooth for a tooth! That's more like it, eh, Doré?"

During those semifinals, our trio arranges itself around the Bakelite box, scarcely daring to speak lest we interfere with the unfolding play-by-play action. Bobby and I miss the ending of the game opener between Wings and Habs because it goes into quadruple overtime and we must attend school the following day; however, when Rocket Richard finally puts the puck past Sawchuk, Grandpa's joyous outpouring wakes the dead: "*Hell's bells! Sacrifice! Doré! Where's your Blinky now? Three full OTs! Then? Boom! Bye-bye Wing Nuts! Aw, Doré, don't worry. At least Blinky ain't bleedin' — yet — and they've still got lots of games to go!*"

Richard clinches Game 2 with a second OT win against Sawchuk, a fact providing Grandpa with further ammunition to prove his point about the departure of goalie Lumley, and although Detroit rallies for a pair at the Olympia, Montreal takes the series with back-to-back wins in Games 5 and 6.

Predictably, Grandpa alternates between ecstatic *told ya so*s, clownish pirouettes complete with jitter-steppin' flourishes and equally annoying postmortems on "them Red Things" with Bobby. Although the stunning Canadien upset smarts, Grandpa takes great pains to delicately rub salt in wounds by gleefully reminding me, a bijillion times a day, *his* Leafs ousted *the* Habs, *the* team that ousted *my* team. *His* Leafs walked all over *my* Wings and returned Stanley to his rightful place as easy as taking candy from a baby.

Naturally, because *his* Leafs recaptured the Cup in 1951, Grandpa's bluster and braggadocio, almost unbearable at the worst of times, nearly drives yours truly to distraction but, like a million fans of a million teams, I counter with that tried and truest of retorts: "Wait until next year, Grandpa. Just wait and see."

The following year, Grandpa's hockey talks border on sermons from the chrome-chair pulpit. In full-flying language the colour of conviction, he holds forth on the pros and princes of his unbeatable Leafs with excruciating affection. He berates my allegiance to an American team, he denigrates Howe's ascending-star status and he ridicules "those stupid guys who don't know the difference between a hockey puck and makin' a buck," especially when one of his guys gets traded "for no good reason. *Sacrifice!*"

By the end of the 1951–52 regular season, Grandpa chalks up the fact Detroit finishes first — and, in the process, literally buries his Leafs — to luck and injuries. The Wings' 100-point season wrap-up doesn't faze him; he simply counters with the team's 101-point failure the previous year.

"Well, Grandpa," I recounter. "Terry Sawchuk had 12 shutouts this year, you know? He'll get that Vézina Trophy, don't you think?"

"The Uke? Yeah, he could do that."

"And the Production Line scored 94 goals, Grandpa."

"Big deal! The Blinky Line? They don't stand a chance unless they do the Stanley dance," he beams, scoring a direct hit on Lindsay's arrogant over-the-head Cup hoist and victory skate following the Wings' impressive 1950

Stanley win (a practice Leaf captain Kennedy cemented as tradition the following year).

Household pandemonium rules prior to the playoffs. Grandpa hits his stride and regularly winds up to fever pitch bragging about his Leafs while bashing away at the competition.

"*Maudit tabernac!*" he hisses. "Montreal don't stand a prayer of a chance…"

"'Course not, Grandpa, Gordie's going to win it for my Wings."

"Who? Blinky? *Sacrifice!* His days is numbered, Doré. 'Sides, ain't he going bald?"

"Wings, Schmings," Bobby pipes up. "Detroit's dead as a doornail on a hot-dog stand."

"Then how come they finished first in the league?"

"Okay, Miss Know-It-All," Grandpa taunts, "who's going to carry your Wings to glory when Blinky makes his next stupid move?"

"Grandpa, Gordie never made his *first* stupid move yet."

"*Pardon?* Go ask Teeder what *he* thinks."

"Grandpa, Teeder sticked Gordie. Gordie *never* made a mistake."

"By the jumpin'! What's this headline say? Listen up. It says, 'Teeder innocent. Blinky guilty. Case closed.'"

"No, it doesn't, Grandpa. It says, 'Some Good Hockey Between Brawls As Wings Tied It.'"

"Yeah? Then what does this one say?"

"'Never A Dull Moment In Leaf–Wing Stanley Cup Game.'"

"Okay. Try this here, then."

"'NHL Head Clears Kennedy.'"

"See! There you go! Teeder innocent. Blinky guilty. Case closed."

Of course, when I can read, I adopt Grandpa's practice of tacking key *Tely* stories outlining particularly stunning Howe feats (and Leaf defeats) to our wall. Stories with glorious Gordie photos Grandpa stands for two or three days before they invariably disappear; photos with rapturous stories Grandpa insists I read from start to finish each time I add a new one.

In between paragraphs, I take great pains to point out the obvious to Grandpa who, as far as I can see, never misses a trick; naturally, as I now see it, Grandpa merely feigns total lack of interest and busily dusts the knobs, dials, glass, top and cord of our radio with his multipurpose hankie to underscore his indifference.

Occasionally, his one and only act of housekeeping accelerates as those now-classic stories wrap up with yet another vindication of the innocence of one triumphant Mr. Howe. When this occurs, Grandpa extracts a dime from his change pouch, removes the screws from the particleboard back of the box and blows emphatically on its rows of pale orange tubes.

"Okay, Grandpa?" I'd ask after winding up for both flourish and finale.

"Yeah, okay," he'd laconically say, "but, know what? I don't care what they say. I know what I saw and I know what *I* say: Your Blinky never told Teeder he was sorry. *Quel toupet!*"

The Howe–Kennedy incident tops Grandpa's list of Wing transgressions and, as such, dominates our friendly feud until it assumes mythic importance as Grandpa's "ace-in-the hole" card, especially when I single out Sawchuk, Kelly, Lindsay, Prystai, et al. for lavish (and deserved) praise.

"Yeah," he grudgingly admits, "they got a few good ones, but, then, they got Blinky! Blinky! He could kill hisself any minute. What kind of player they got there, eh? *Sacrebleu!*"

Whether Grandpa would or could ever openly acknowledge Howe's stunning five-decade contribution to the NHL (with Detroit and the Hartford Whalers), I do not know. I do know, with the luxury of hindsight, what kind of player he became by the time he retired at 52: the finest all-round hockeyist in the history of the game.

So I shall never forget Grandpa's everlasting chagrin when unstoppable 1952 Red Wings roll past the Leafs in the semi-finals and Habs in the finals to snag Stanley on a straight-eight (Octopus) ticket, a striking achievement made all the more spectacular by Sawchuk's unparalleled performance in goal that unforgettable season he breaks all standing records.

Those untarnished games of consummate perfection still shine in my mind; a watershed of civilization and supreme knowledge all proceeds apace with Howe, hockey, our little house on Church Street and one young Wingster enraptured with the stunning feats of a handful of truly extraordinary mortals.

From the opening frame, the sound of puck colliding with solid wood promising a singular series of outstanding achievements, Grandpa and I sit glued to our moods and track each remarkable accomplishment with reverence, respect and inexplicable awe. After all, my "Red Things" slay all contenders and outplay all pretenders with smarts, sass, savvy and a sheer burning love of the game, passion for perfection and will to win still unequalled in professional sports.

And although Howe doesn't score a goal in the Leaf semifinal, he scores five in the final against the Habs, a fact that nearly drives Grandpa to distraction. In Game 2 of that series, Howe characteristically checks a Dollard St. Laurent charge by bestowing a lacerated eyeball on the upstart. (Equally characteristically, he helps the injured Canadien off the ice.)

Of course, Grandpa particularly relishes the fights, the fisticuffs, the down-and-dirty deviltry of a few dozen champions proving their prowess. In full-force conversation with disembodied voices, we simply sit, watch and listen to his inexhaustible running commentary punctuated by fists blasting imaginary jaws and hands clutching imaginary sticks only he can see in that Church Street kitchen. He swings his lefts, jabs his rights and hooks the air while engaging in some of the fastest chair-dancing footwork on the planet.

Each time Howe puts the puck past Jacques Plante or Gerry McNeil, Grandpa bangs his chair against the rag rug placed strategically beneath rubber-tipped feet and sends butts into orbit with a bright orange Canada Tavern ashtray, and valour drowns discretion in the outpouring: "*Sacrebleu!* Those Frenchies need a better guy! Those guys need Béliveau, the only player who can outshoot ol' stinky Blinky!"

"Grandpa," I insist, "Blinky isn't stinky."

He twitches his nose. "P-U! I can smell the guy from here."

☆

Thus, when we take up our positions in the off-limits living room — Grandpa in his chair, Bobby sprawled on the floor and me on the hassock near the chrome pedestal ashtray a foot or so from the new television — we stare at the green screen in anticipation of tiny tabletop hockey players coming to life on its other side and settle in for Game 1 of the 1952–53 semifinal between Detroit and Boston.

In inimitable fashion, Grandpa tells me not to get my hopes up: first, he points out, Detroit lacks depth; second, Blinky's slipping after working so hard in the regular season (and *still* missing the 50-goal mark by one); finally, Boston will shut the Production Line down *and* even though Delvecchio did score the league's shooter title *and* even though Red Kelly never looked better *and* even with Pronovost playing his heart out, *aujour-d'hui roi, demain rien.*

Sometimes, when Grandpa shoots his mouth off, he scores; and sometimes, when Detroit doesn't live up to our expectations, he resorts to lessons about lesser players whom he believes will give Howe a run for his money.

That year, he favoured Max Bentley, "the farm boy from Saskatchewan who got good 'cause the little scrapper had the will to win."

"Gordie's got it too, Grandpa. Gordie comes from Saskatchewan, you know?"

"Yeah, the guy comes from *Floral!*"

"Yeah, but he moved to Saskatoon when he turned nine, Grandpa!"

"Yeah? Did he milk the cows, then?"

"Cows?"

"Yeah, Max milked cows in Saskatchewan."

"Naw, Grandpa, Gordie lived in skates and practised all

the time, summer and winter, day in and day out."

"Yeah? Did you know his folks was poor? They couldn't even buy him a new pair of skates."

"Yeah, but his mom got him a used pair he stuffed with newspapers. He just wanted to play hockey so bad. And he got so good."

"Did not."

"Grandpa, Gordie just won the H…"

"Hoogaw Trophy? That trophy they give to those guys that tell lies?"

"Grandpa!"

"Well? Did your Gordie tell *the truth?*"

"'Course, Grandpa. Did your Teddy?"

"*Pardon?*"

"Teddy…Teddy *Kennedy.* Did *Teddy* tell the truth, Grandpa?"

"By the jumpin'…"

To this day, I still gag when I see a bar of green Palmolive soap and recall his threat to wash my mouth out with same.

☆

Two seasons later, with my Wings in stellar form and Grandpa's Leafs on the rebuild trail, he confidently predicts a shake-up showdown. In a way, he prognosticates correctly, except the showdown takes place between Habs and Wings (after Detroit destroys his Leafs in the semifinals).

"*Bien,*" says Grandpa, "*très bien.* Now, watch what I mean. Those Frenchies finally got Béliveau."

"And Gordie just won his fourth straight scoring title, Grandpa."

"*Pas de problème,* Doré."

"Wanna bet?"

Back and forth goes the 1954–55 series. Wings win the first. Habs take the second. Wings nab the third. Habs tie it. Wings win the fifth. Again, Habs tie it. And so it goes right down to the wire: Wings and Habs face off for the seventh game before an overflow crowd at the Olympia, and, when Detroit's Tony Leswick drops the puck over McNeil's shoulder with the unexpected help of Canadien defenceman Doug Harvey in the fifth minute of overtime, Wings hoist the Cup and disheartened Habs leave the ice without the traditional handshakes, a gesture beyond Grandpa's comprehension.

"Doré, that's the meanest thing I ever saw. Didn't Wings just win that regular-season crown? Ain't Wings the best team d'hockey? Ain't they got Gordie?"

"Yup, Grandpa, Wings got Gordie."

Thus, when President Campbell suspends Richard for the three remaining games (and the playoffs) the following season, Grandpa's only comment, the one I shall never forget?

"The Rocket lost it."

After *the* riot and the anti-climactic playoffs, my Wings beat Montreal fair and square. Even Grandpa says so.

"*Sacrebleu!* Them Wings closed their case…"

"…and Gordie nailed it shut, eh, Grandpa?"

"Yup, ol' stinky Blinky couldn't have played better. He even shook hands with the Rocket!"

"Yup, Grandpa, Gordie played the best!"

"Yup, Doré, Gordie played the best."

Looking back, I recall Saturday evenings in the Church of Hockey Night in Canada with a mixture of bemusement and gratitude. I spent time with an extraordinary character who taught *the truth* in astonishingly simple terms: "*Aujourd'hui roi, demain rien.*" Several decades later, my photograph of Grandpa standing in front of Betsy, his beautiful beat-up Buick, still hangs at eye level on my kitchen wall, right next to our favourite picture of Gordie, the one where the finest player in the history of the game first touches the cherished Cup, grinning deliriously, shorn skull and all.

As of this writing, the Detroit Red Wings have not won the Stanley Cup since 1955. — Ed.

4

THE BOSTON BRUINS

BY PAUL QUARRINGTON

I AM THINKING ABOUT SPACE. WHERE I WAS BORN WAS nothing but space, stretched from one end of the Earth to the other, unchanged and unchanging, except for a few pinches and folds like wrinkles in a bed sheet. That is where I was a boy and young man, and I have formulated a theory that of all the years in a life, it is these that are most causative as regards breed and stamp. So I am not merely thinking about space, I am feeling space as an absence and a hunger.

Here on Brookline Avenue in Boston, Massachusetts, on January 2, 1929, I am caught in terrible traffic. I am sitting in the backseat of a taxicab, and all around us are sleek black machines, shivering in the frigid night. The driver of my car is beset with nervousness. His gloved hands clutch the rim of the steering wheel; he shifts his fat rump about

Eddie Shore

on the seat so that the chilled leather sends up shrieks and howls. He is apprehensive, I'm sure, that I will count this all as his fault and do him harm. I find this almost humorous in its unaccountability, although I suppose I did enter the cab with a sort of swirling menace, muttering darkly that I must get to the railway station.

Like all of Boston and much of the world, the driver attributes to me a dull-witted ferocity. But the swirling, you know, had mostly to do with my cape, for I had been dining at the home of Xanthus Goodnough, and he had, as per usual, set the tone high. I am wearing a suit of the deepest black, complemented by this long cape. It would prove unsatisfactory protection against the winter, to an ordinary man. But where I come from, coldness, frigidity, is King Stork.

What the driver read for menace is merely annoyance, with myself for overstaying a party I did not enjoy and with Bruins general manager Art Ross for no better reason than he sets the schedules, so although he is as blameless as the clock itself, I am annoyed with him.

Every so often the driver will work the pedals and levers, the cab will shudder and leap forward a yard or so. In this manner we have progressed half a city block and have achieved the convergence with Beacon Road. Suddenly the root of all this trouble is evident. Two of the metal beasts have clashed and tangled. They entered the open ground at Kenmore Square without heed or caution, and now they are both twisted and useless. One of the drivers lies awkwardly upon the ground. His driving goggles are misted, even in the night's chilled bitterness, as though his eyes had given off a blast of great radiance. His hat remains carefully arranged upon his head. Beside him lies a wedge of glass from the windscreen, and it has opened his throat. People stand about and gawk, immobilized by the sight of blood, even though blood is the most basic and precious of humours. I would stop and help, but beyond the accident is space, at least a bit more blessed space. I urge the driver to hurry; he executes a very military-style salute and we fly away toward the railway station.

Ross demands that the railway give us the very last sleeper on the train, his averred reason being that, like lepers or convicts, hockey players must be segregated from more genteel folk. This is not meant as humour, although my teammates will pop their eyes open and issue great barks of laughter whenever they hear it. I know Ross better than they; he intends no irony at all, but on this night I applaud his choice, because at least I have a chance. Which is to say, the train has left the station. It is some 200 yards down the tracks and, as they say, gathering steam, although the stack throws off so much of the stuff as to put a lie to that terminology. Vapour explodes into the air and is frozen into clouds of such solidity you could saw them into pieces.

I run with all the vigour I can summon, my black cape fanning out behind me and flapping with the urgency and tone of a snare drum. But running seems ineffectual, too puny and mechanical, and I realize suddenly that hoarfrost clings to the world and will allow something that resembles skating. And this is best how to navigate about the globe, your legs spread so as to take in some of its roundness, the centre of your being closer to the core of the planet. My opponents often deride my skating style, claiming that it is awkward, splay-legged like the hockey stride of a child. I do not, in truth, deny this, but it behooves me to strike these men down whenever I can.

☆ THE BOSTON BRUINS ☆

And if I was given to cursing, I would surely curse my shoes, because they were made for no purpose other than to sheathe my feet in pebbled leather and to hide their horny nakedness in presentable company and are useless upon the wintry ground. Even so, the backside of the train draws momentarily nearer. But then I lose footing — if one can lose what one never had — and I go down.

My problems were caused by machines — the bullheaded sedans that roared into the paved arena, neither giving way — so I look to machines for the answer. Having ascertained from the stationmaster that there are no further trains scheduled for Montreal, Quebec — he offered this information apologetically, perhaps, like the cab driver, fearing my wrath — I demand to use a telephone. I inform the operator that I wish to communicate with Boston Airfield. He briefly tries to cajole more specific information, but I feel that I have been helpful enough.

A connection is made.

"This is Edward Shore," I speak. "It is essential that I charter an airplane. I need to get to Montreal."

"But Mr. Shore," returns the person on the other end (the voice is strangled by the thin wires; I do not know whether it belongs to man or woman), "no airplanes are flying tonight."

"Why is that?"

"Because of the storm."

My head jerks up, I search out the black windows. I nod and cradle the earpiece without speaking. The storm has not yet reached Boston, but suddenly I feel it, the movement of the cold air due to riotous changes in electric and magnetic modalities.

I have reasons for needing to be in Montreal. The Bruins record stands at six wins, seven losses and a pair of ties, miserable by my reckoning, merely mediocre by the league's. A victory or two would alter the whole complexion of the campaign. So that is one reason I must be in Montreal. Also, we are already down a spare, Dit Clapper having received a puck to the head, which broke open his skull, and although he suffers no greater malady today than bleary vision, the doctors have forbidden him to play. So that is yet another reason why I must be in Montreal.

But the best reason has to do with the storm, which will not stop me.

☆

He, Nathan, is of a sort I don't much care for. He is large and uncontained; I can detect beneath his overcoat unformed bulges, indicating too much drink and fried food. He affects a moustache, but only a handful of hairs have sprouted upon his upper lip. Nathan wears them anyway, testimonial to a manhood that is suspect and feckless. He waddles into the railway station, plants his splayed feet, takes a long look around. The cap upon his head, the symbol of livery and servitude, he neglects to remove.

He has come at the behest of his employer, Xanthus Goodnough, chief sanitary engineer for the city of Boston. I count Goodnough as a friend, despite his overly affected manners and the uncustomary food he serves for dinner, tiny birds and outgrown vegetative matter. What I like about Xanthus, I suspect, is the fact that he has embarked upon a quest — the search for a new water supply for the metropolis — and has vision enough to pursue it fearlessly and in all quarters, beneath the Earth's crust, at the lightless bottom of the sea.

Having ascertained, therefore, that there were neither trains nor airplanes (none that were willing to fly through the mounting tempest), I instructed the operator to make contact with Goodnough.

"This is Shore."

"Edward? Did you forget something?"

There were noises in the background that rendered his words indistinct. It seemed that I could hear shrieking and laughter more suited to a lunatic asylum, although the gathering I departed was a dour affair.

"I missed my train."

"Ha!" laughed Goodnough. "Ross shall have your testes with his tea. Oh, dear. Well, come back here, then. We're having the grandest fun ever."

"You have a driver? An automobile and a driver?"

"Yes, tell me where you are, he shall come gather you up."

"Send me an automobile and a driver. I'm going to Montreal."

Now Nathan enters the railway station and takes a look around. "Shore?" he demands loudly.

I rise from the bench, pull the black cape around my shoulders. "Let's go," I say.

☆

We are creeping along the Mystic River valley. The snow has commenced but seems harmless enough. Nathan considers this an unremarkable drive, as his attitude indicates. He sits low in the seat, his shoulders sunken, working pedals and levers with patent disinterest. I know that the snow is far from harmless, because where I come from, winter is King Stork. I see that the flakes are fat and misshapen; they are delivered from a distant polar vortex.

"Canada," Nathan muses aloud.

"Eh?"

"Canada," he repeats. "I've never been there. I've always wanted to see it. I've heard it's very pretty."

I do not respond to any of these merely declarative utterances. Nathan, I think, bristles at my silence. "You're Canadian," he says in an accusatory fashion, craning his neck so that he can stare at me in the backseat, as if to see if I looked different from others. I wave at the road ahead, which twists alongside the Mystic. "That is correct," I answer.

"Your King is sick," he announces.

"I'm sorry?"

"The King of the British Commonwealth. The monarch of your country. George the, uh…" Nathan removes one hand from the steering wheel and silently counts off fingers. "Fifth. He has toxemia."

I point a finger toward the windshield. "Look. Notice how the snowflakes, for all their size, lack substance. As soon as they hit the glass, they disappear in a state of dissolution. In the mountains there will be chaos."

As if to mollify me, Nathan is silent for a moment or two and applies his concentration to the road. "Know who else is sick?"

"Who?"

"Leon Trotsky."

"I'm unacquainted with the man."

"Yeah." Nathan reaches upward and twists the windshield-cleaner regulating valve. The wiper-blade swoops down but skitters uselessly across the glass.

"Ice," say I.

The word is no sooner spoken than the car twists and yaws. Suddenly we are spinning on the dark road, looking into the forests, looking into the river, into the trees, into the Mystic. Nathan turns the wheel almost casually and somehow manages to pull the automobile back into its tracks. Having done that, he applies the brake pedal and pulls the Cadillac off to the side of the road.

Nathan is panting like an old dog that has been left out in the sun. He removes his chauffeur's cap and nervously thumbs the lining as though some message might be secreted away.

"What the hell just happened?" Nathan whispers.

"You were driving too fast."

"It was like…"

"Oh, I know what it was like, pal. I know very well what it was like."

☆

Nathan has been silent for the past little while, concentrating on his duties as chauffeur. Despite the temperature — which has plummetted and sent wintry air particles into a turmoil — he has broken a sweat. Little beads cling to the sparse hairs of his moustache.

"I've got to tell you, Shore, this is tough going. Wouldn't you rather be home in bed?"

"I have made a decision."

"To turn back?"

"No, no. To get to Montreal."

"You maybe did, but I never."

Suddenly there are lights ahead, a small outpost. We do not know what lies beyond. Maps may have various cross-hatchings, perhaps an artist has etched pictures of mountains, looking as orderly and civilized as a row of felt hats, but this is all bluff and veneer. As are maps of where I come from. There the cartographers content themselves with taking a straight rule and scratching out a box, slightly fatter at the bottom than it is at the top. They carefully print words in the emptiness, but that is weak medicine and does not help.

Nathan says, "I never made any decision. You did." He has repositioned his statements, as if my lack of a response had to do with points of logic or grammar.

I nod toward the lights, a quarter of a mile distant. "Turn in up there."

Nathan eagerly depresses the accelerator pedal, and I am forced to grab him by the shoulder. "Do not drive more quickly. Maintain a moderate forward heading. Concentrate upon your mission…"

"That hurts, you know." Nathan jerks his head, a spasm that brings his chin and the rolls of pale fat that lie beneath it near my hand momentarily.

"That hurts?"

"Yes."

I slowly release the fingers and push myself back into the seat.

There is a gas pump, cocooned with ice. A display of cans containing oils and lubricants has been knocked over by a petulant wind. The sign over the top of the edifice is only half-lit, the beam for the right half either long dead or recently snuffed out by the storm. It says, Lincoln's Motor Service. We roll to a stop in the middle of the lot. Nathan places his thumb upon the horn button and sends a howl into the heartless night.

"What are you doing?" I ask him.

"Getting the guy," he snaps.

"I'll get the guy." I push open the door and emerge from the automobile.

It is cold inside the cab, certainly, but nothing like out here. I find myself with my nose held slightly aloft, as though sniffing out prey, but truly I am only trying to gauge the bite, the severity of the cold. I have had my nose frostbitten many times, so many times that by the age of 12 my nose was bluish with broken veins and appeared to be grog-blossomed. I gather the extremities of my cape into my hands and raise my arms; the wind makes of it wings. I turn a circle in the middle of the asphalt, each step ginger and light, as though I am dancing with a strange woman and am fearful of trodding upon her dainty feet.

I see that Nathan is hunched over and staring at me through the windows. "Not that bad," I call out to him. "It may be even melting in the high ground." I wave toward the blackness and turn away before he challenges this falsehood.

The door to the establishment repeats its proclamation, Lincoln's Motor Service, and here someone has added a portrait of that particular president, a rather crude effort that takes advantage of black paint, atoning for a vagueness about the eyes, nose and mouth with a severe chin-strap beard and a popped top hat. Without these appurtenances, of course, the man in the painting would look no more like Honest Abe than do I. I study the painting briefly. Indeed, without these appurtenances, the man in the painting would resemble Ross.

I hammer upon the door, which opens almost immediately. A lamp hovers there, clutched in a dark, wrinkled hand. A black man peers beyond it suspiciously, his eyes narrowed, trying to make me out. He holds a book in the other hand, his thumb driven between the pages, holding the spot. He has, I see, but a few pages to go.

"What?"

"We need gasoline," I tell him, "and chains."

He lowers the lamp and takes in my aspect slowly. He looks over and sees Nathan in the automobile. Then he makes a brief survey of the world outside. "You want to drive in *this?*" he asks. He seems surprised to see that it is storming. Perhaps he has been reading his book for days, hunched in an easy chair in a windowless room.

For some reason I take some care in my answer, even though it was thrown at me in a distracted manner, the questioner really not all that interested. But I take care, as though he were empowered to stop me. "We want to drive," I speak slowly. "*This* just happens to be here."

Nathan is ignorant as to the process of putting on chains. This makes him defensive and standoffish. Having climbed out of the car, responding reluctantly to my request for assistance, he takes three or four large strides away and then turns to watch as I crouch beside the wheels. A cigarette protrudes from between his fat, pale lips.

I lay out the chains upon the frozen ground. "You see what you have to do? Lay them out like this, and then motor the automobile forward two feet, then we'll…"

"Who says I have to do anything?" demands Nathan. The wind has knocked the ember out of his smoke and rendered it lifeless, despite which he takes a great haul as he stares at me. "I am not your employee. I work for Xanthus Goodnough. I am also not chattel he can loan out to his rich friends."

"Fair enough. Give me the key to the switch lock."

"Why?"

"So that I may proceed upon my journey."

"What am I supposed to do?"

"You can wait here. I'll be back through the day after tomorrow. Or you can come with me."

Something like a smile comes to Nathan's lips. He heads for the automobile and climbs into the back.

"Think about your man Mackenzie King," says Nathan, reclining in the passenger's seat and drawing on a fresh cigarette. "It is bad enough that he dances to somebody else's tune. What's worse, there are two men beating drums."

I grunt, to no real purpose, it is simply a sound I make in the silence as I stare through the darkened windscreen. The snow is now frenzied; it no longer toes and slants from the heavenly vault, now it charges head-on, some even circles and flutters upward, like sparks from a bonfire. The rime settles upon the blacktop, a blanket of glistening silver. The whole world appears frozen, and I have a sudden vision of everyone, the entire populace, playing a game of shinny, each of us wearing a jersey emblazoned with a different letter, emblem or image of an animal.

Here and there the wind has collected snow into small burial cairns. I try to avoid these, but the headlights do not pick them out until they are near, and I am also fearful of pulling the car too quickly out of the path. So some I hit and for an instant I am powerless; the car shimmies and shakes; I am trapped inside the machine and powerless. This is why I make a grunt. Nathan interprets it to best serve his own needs.

"Why, Coolidge and Baldwin, of course."

A small decline now, the beginnings of the black mountains. The car slips downward eagerly, like a diver from the Brooklyn Bridge. I pull back upon the wheel, foolishly I suppose, as if I could rein in a wild beast. The car straightens and begins to climb again. The next ascent is longer.

☆

Nathan is saying this: "The governments of greed and tyranny," the first time I lose all control of the automobile. It is surprising, too, because I had been expecting the front of the car to go wild, pressing my fingers lightly on the steering wheel, as though they held reins, and concentrating just a few feet beyond the windscreen. But it is the rear that bucks, kicking up off a drift and then never settling upon the roadway, wheeling to the right and dropping into the ditch. The engine groans and whimpers. There are oil fumes and thin weeds of black smoke.

I climb out of the car and look into the back. Nathan has been disarranged, thrown against the side of the passenger compartment. There is a thin trickle of blood descending from his mouth. I rap hard upon the glass with my knuckles.

"I need help."

Nathan makes no move to join me outside the automobile. Instead, he reaches over with a hand and works the window lever furiously, pushing the glass with his other hand when it will not descend quickly enough to suit his anger. "Goddamn it, Shore," says Nathan, "can't you see I'm hurt?"

"You've bitten your own tongue."

"We've had an accident," he explains. Nathan reaches up and pats his forehead, searching for more flows of blood.

"The hind end is in a ditch, that's all. We've got to push it out."

"You'd better stop telling me things I have to do."

Sometimes there is a darkness that comes upon me, a wordless energy that occupies my brain, and I must act, which is to say, *perform some action,* or be overwhelmed and consumed by it. I might, for example, notice all my teammates clustered and loitering about the enemy net, awaiting errant pucks, and instead of annoyance comes this darkness. Then I must launch myself away, scraping the ice with the metal blades until it shrieks and howls, taking the puck with me only as an afterthought. When I attain scoring range, my teammates will hunch over their sticks and holler, "Eddie!" but I ignore them. They are no longer part of it. Neither are the opposites nor the man between the pipes. By then it is just between me and the darkness. The tally often calms me somewhat.

What I do now is hurl myself into the ditch, jumping with such force that the fresh snow curls up around my knees. I double the cape across my right shoulder and place the shoulder against the rear bumper. I push and even as Nathan pops his head through the window and says, "Don't be stupid, that's impossible," the car rolls forward and the back end swings obediently back into its ruts. I leap out of the ditch and brush at the snow. But I am not too thorough; I enjoy the bite of the frozen stones melting upon my hot skin.

☆

There is a truck slumbering by the side of the road, shrouded with snow, draped with icicles. I pull over just beyond it and ignore Nathan's whine, "What are you doing now, Shore?" because he doesn't truly care. I step out of the car. The wind has abated somewhat here in the folds of the mountains, although I can hear it howling above in the blackened canopy. I walk back to the truck and jump upon the running board. The truck rocks, and with the first pitch a face appears at the window, round and white and frightened. The face recedes into the darkness and then comes again. This time effort has been made to compose the features with placidity. The eyes have soft, dark bags both below and above, indicative of a lack of vitamins and nutriments.

The door is opened a crack so that we might talk.

"You riding it out by the side of the road, are you, pal?"

"Of course I am," he answers. He blinks constantly, but without rhythm or system, his purpled eyelids twitching. "What are *you* doing?"

"Trying to get to Montreal, P.Q."

"And why would you be trying to do that?"

"Because I have a feeling that the Maroons might yield to us a couple of points. But they must be met and engaged."

Blinking all the while, the man allows his puffy eyes to

take in the whole of my visage. "Eddie Shore," he says lowly. "The 'Babe' Ruth of hockey."

"Babe Ruth," I return, "is the Eddie Shore of baseball."

The man laughs, and his eyes close completely. For a moment I am staring at two swollen, bruised, blind circles.

"Buddy," I continue, "do you have a shovel? A shovel and maybe an axe? I'll buy them from you."

"Forget it," he says, blinking once more.

"Fair enough."

"Hell," says the truck driver, "I'll give them to you."

And this is fortunate, for as we near the mountains' crests, the wind is emboldened by its proximity to the heavens and the automobile is pushed sideways off the road, just as a petulant child might slap away a wooden car.

I take the shovel and axe and step out. The tires are buried in the deep snow, which I cannot help but admire. The snow is moonlit and thus rendered silver. I have not asked Nathan to assist and am surprised to hear the passenger door open. He lights into it gingerly, testing the snow with his toe, as though he were stepping into bathwater.

"This is a fine predicament."

I shrug, I grunt, jerk my head in a fashion that is neither a nod nor a shake. In truth, I do not know precisely what I do, only that it seems to anger Nathan. "We could die out here," he exclaims in an overly dramatic fashion. "Did you ever think of that?"

"No," I reply truthfully, tossing a bladeful of heavy, wet snow over my shoulder.

"Well, we could," he insists.

"We need traction and leverage." I stab the shovel into the drifts and leave it standing like a flag or marker, exchanging it for the axe. "I saw a little thicket about a quarter of a mile back. I'll be back in a bit."

And when I return, dragging the twisted limbs of an old cedar behind me, Nathan is resting beside the shovel and smoking yet another cigarette. He has dug out around the car, although the scoop marks are small, infrequent and ginger, like what a dowager might leave behind in a bowlful of spiced chili. I arrange the branches before and beneath the tires.

As Nathan works the levers, I press from the rear. We free the automobile and continue toward the north.

In the crest of the mountains, the night is its blackest, the storm perhaps its worst, despite which Nathan is blabbering, naming the names of powerful and evil men. Then there is a brief respite, and when his voice comes again, it is louder, coarser.

"Jesus, Shore, you don't say very much, do you?"

"I don't talk as much as you, that's true. I'm not as frightened as you are."

Nathan takes umbrage. "I think perhaps you just don't really comprehend what I'm saying. I'm talking about political systems, after all, and you're just an athlete."

"Huh."

"I don't suppose you read many books."

"Is that what you don't suppose?"

"I read all the time. The great works of philosophy. Karl Marx. Hegel."

The wiper is now useless, dulled by overwork and twisted by the wind. Every few moments it will fall upon the sheet of grainy ice that claims the glass, it will scratch out a thin half smile, which, for a few moments, I can peer through. I espy the clasps on either side of the top pane. Holding fast to the steering wheel with my right hand, I raise my left and press the mechanism immediately beside me. The bolt and sheathe are so cold they are almost frozen together, and the force required to pop the one out of the other is such that it fills not only my thumb but the whole of my arm with pain.

I speak now as much to rest my arm, briefly, as to communicate with Nathan. "I, too, read all the time. But I read books of practical value."

"Such as?"

"Such as medical books."

"Oh, studying to be a doctor, Shore?"

"Studying so as to have as little to do with doctors as possible."

"Oh, yeah."

"Doctors deal with sick and diseased bodies. I want to learn about one that is strong and healthy."

My left arm now has enough feeling that I can flex the fingers, so I position it upon the rim of the wheel and reach out with my right. The bolt over there comes out more easily, and the top pane of glass folds over with much clatter, and the wind is suddenly inside the car.

"What in the name of God are you doing?"

"This is the only way I can see." The storm lays its icy hand upon my face and tries to close my eyes.

The farmer and his wife seem surprised to see me. This might have as much to do with the colour of my face as anything, with the fact that my eyebrows and lashes are laden with white crystal. They had been preparing break-fast; many lamps are lit, guiding the way for these people from the night into the dawn. Perhaps I am a bit delirious, because for a long moment all I can do is smile, somehow stirred by this scene of tranquillity.

The farmer says, "Yes?" and I wave toward the road, more waving than is absolutely necessary.

"Do you have dray horses or mules I could borrow for a moment? I seem to have driven into yet another ditch."

In the late morning the storm breaks. There is a rift between the banks of purpled clouds, and the snow is transformed. There is peace enough in the atmosphere that the flakes dance, like tiny angels. There is warmth enough that the black ice upon the tarmac softens and yields. The tires settle upon it and hold surely.

I have eyes left, and that's all I can be sure of. Everything else is numb. I know I have eyes because I have sight, although even that was lost several times during the night, the lids frozen shut. When feeling returns to my body, I shall be wracked with pain, fired with anguish, and I hope the timing works out so that I am upon the ice at that time, because I will dominate and destroy. My com-munion with the storm has strengthened my spirit, even if it has weakened the flesh.

Speaking of which, I must seek slumber.

I pull over to the side of the road.

Nathan is sleeping behind me. His mouth hangs open and a tiny snail of spit trails from a corner of his pale lips. "Nathan." I have only to speak his name and he awakens, alarmed and panicky. Nathan has been destroyed, at least a small part of him, and he and the night shall never be on close terms.

"You have to drive now."

"I can't…"

"Please. I'm not telling you to, I'm asking you to."

"Sure, but Eddie, I'm afraid."

"Maintain a moderate forward heading. Do not exceed 25 miles per hour. We are now on the road for Montreal. The border is just up ahead."

"Well…" He hesitates.

"These men you speak of. The men that you claim rule the world. They don't. They are petty despots, paper kings. Like Ross. They have a little control, got through fear and money. But Nathan…" I press my face close to his. "Nathan, *winter* is King Stork. All the power of men is nothing compared to a good northern blow. And when we arrive in Montreal, Nathan, then we can say…I always hesitate on the brink of indelicacy.

"We can say *fuck you.*" Nathan understands me now.

"That is correct."

Nathan adjusts his chauffeur's cap eagerly.

I wrap my black cape around me tightly, close my eyes and drift away.

There are moments of connection, when the way, or a portion of it, is lighted through this dark vale, and this moment just before darkness is one. I see tomorrow's newspaper — *Shore Beats Maroons 1–0* — and a thin smile curls my lips.

Then comes sleep.

General Manager Arthur H. Ross fined Eddie Shore
$500 for missing the train. — Ed.

5

THE TORONTO MAPLE LEAFS

BY TRENT FRAYNE

IT IS AN EARLY-SPRING MORNING LIKE MOST EARLY-SPRING mornings, a damp and overcast April day in 1985, and Pat Muldoon has a mood to match the grey morning. Muldoon has tottered into Maple Leaf Gardens hoping for a painless interview. He is feeling every one of his 62 years as he shuffles toward the little coffee shop inside. If one of the players drops by after the team's morning skate, he'll grab him and ask some penetrating question like "What's the matter with the Leafs?" Muldoon grunts sourly. His disposition is low because his hangover is ouching. Also because the team is going so lousy. Who wants to read about them? Not for the first time Muldoon wonders if he's been at his game too long, if he has written too many columns for the Toronto *World*. What was it somebody wrote? "With athletes the legs go

King Clancy

first; with sportswriters it's the enthusiasm." Yeah.

Muldoon buys his coffee, blows on the steam rising from the cup and glances around. Four secretaries from the Gardens offices upstairs are into hushed talk and a midmorning snack. Workers in bulky blue-and-white sweaters mumble quietly at another table. Muldoon knows that in the old days this place would be buzzing — visiting writers, four or five scouts, television guys. Muldoon shakes his head. Nothing has been the same for the Maple Leafs since Harold Ballard took over. For 15 years they haven't licked their lips.

And Ballard's such a schmuck. Like the time young Johnny Bassett put the old Toronto Toros into the Gardens when the World Hockey Association was trying to find its legs. Ballard gave them nothing. One night, with practically nobody in the rink, Ballard noticed that the Toronto players had their bottoms on a long narrow cushion that covered the bench. He told a workman to get down there and roust the Toros off the cushion and store it in the Leaf dressing room. Ballard chuckled, watching the workman tell the players to lift their butts.

The Leafs, as usual, were stumbling, last in their division. Ballard had dumped Darryl Sittler, the former star centre who had fallen from favour, calling him a cancer in the lineup. He said Inge Hammarstrom was a typical Swede: "If he went into the corner carrying eggs, he'd come out with none of 'em cracked." In an interview with the widely respected broadcaster Barbara Frum, Ballard called her "a dumb broad" and told her that women were "only good for lying on their backs." One time he loudly called a writer a fag. Ballard was a lulu, all right.

Muldoon grows depressed thinking about Ballard. He needs a drink. He looks at his watch, 20 minutes past 10, and is ready to take off when suddenly there at the doorway is King Clancy bouncing into the coffee shop. "Well now, the top o' the mornin' to one and all," Clancy calls merrily, his lantern jaw preceding him into the room by three or four inches. He glances toward the table where the secretaries sit. "An' especially good mornin' to the ladies there with the charmin' eyes." He dances a little jig, then leaps into the air, clicking his heels on the right side, then jumps again and clicks them on the left.

On this gloomy April morning King Clancy is 82 years old.

"King," Muldoon calls. "Got a minute?"

Muldoon knows it is Clancy's spirit, his happy outlook, his warmth, his decency, his enthusiasm, even his ear-rattling profanity that have always made people glad they haven't missed him. All his life Clancy has been a kid at heart. If anything hurts, he doesn't bother saying so. He doesn't carry grudges. One decent thing Ballard has done is to keep Clancy on at the Gardens. Except for occasional forays to the farm club in Pittsburgh, Pennsylvania, where he coached, and a decade of refereeing, where he was the

NHL's best, Clancy has spent much of his adult life in and around the Gardens. He's been there as a player and a coach and, in his later years, as the vice-president in charge of making everybody feel good.

Clancy's ebullient spirit has been a force around the building almost from the moment Conn Smythe shelled out the astronomical sum of $35,000, plus two players, to land him from the Ottawa Senators on the eve of the 1930–31 season. The Senators needed the money or they never would have permitted the departure of the fiery chatterbox often called "150 pounds of muscle and conversation," a runt of five feet seven inches and tough as a cheap steak.

"D'ye want a coffee?" Clancy calls now to the newspaperman.

"No, no, I'm fine. I just want to talk a minute."

Watching Clancy as he orders the coffee, Muldoon feels his sour mood beginning to lift. It is impossible to stay down for long in the company of the merry little fellow. Even when Clancy was a referee, he made people laugh, a rare achievement for someone in that line of work. Muldoon recalls the Stanley Cup final of 1945 when Clancy was in charge of the seventh and deciding game in the steaming cauldron of the old Detroit Olympia.

The Red Wings were seeking to even matters for a humiliation they had endured three springs earlier in Toronto. Back then, the Wings had a firm grip on the

Stanley Cup; they'd hammered favoured Toronto in the opening three games of the final series and then, for the only time in hockey history, had lost the next four games.

Now, though, they were about to wipe out that irritating piece of lore. The Maple Leafs, playing stultifying defensive hockey in front of their ulcerated goaltender, Frank McCool, won the first three games of this 1945 final by 1–0, 2–0 and 1–0 scores. But then the Red Wings answered some distant alarm clock and brought down the Leafs by 5–3, 2–0 and 1–0 and were now at home in their own raucous arena for the biggest game of all. The man assigned to handle matters in this tension-packed situation was the league's best referee, a man named King Clancy.

And though he was a former Maple Leaf kingpin, there was no question of Clancy being partial to the Leafs. Indeed, he may even have been leaning a trifle sideways, if not backward, in the third period while the Leafs were holding grimly to a 1–0 lead. In rapid succession he sent two of them to the penalty box, and the Leaf coach, Hap Day, and their defensive stalwart, Babe Pratt, were particularly hot in arguing against Clancy's calls. Indeed, Pratt, tall and erect, had barbered with Clancy all season whenever their paths crossed, each of them a noted enemy of silence.

Now, with the crowd up and roaring in the hot, smokey broiler of a rink, the Leafs, playing two men short, struggled to hold off the assault. As the Wing players stormed in, Pratt, stick extended, backing toward goal-tender McCool, bumped Clancy, briefly setting him off-stride. Clancy wasn't sure but that it was a deliberate bump and he whirled on Pratt.

"Ye son of a buck, I'd like to be playin' against ye tonight!" he growled.

Pratt looked down at little Clancy. "Well," he said inno-cently enough, glancing at his two teammates in the penal-ty box, "aren't you?"

Now, in the coffee shop, King grins good-naturedly when Pat Muldoon reminds him of Pratt's needle.

"He was a fine fella, that Babe," Clancy says. "Ye know, he worked on the railway in the offseason to keep in shape. We used to call him the Honest Switchman because he never stole a boxcar."

At which point Muldoon, still hoping for an easy col-umn, turns to current matters.

"Your team looks terrible," he says bluntly. "What's the problem?"

Clancy frowns. "Ah, the damned game's not the same, you know that," he tells Muldoon. "We don't have a soul who'll walk out there tonight when the whistle blows and hammer somebody into the seats. They're all thinkin' about their money, I guess. If we had some dirty son of a bitch like Sprague Cleghorn who'd just go out there and kick the bejesus out of somebody, I tell ye we'd win the damn Stanley Cup." Clancy's scarred and mobile old kisser is creased in gloom. "But we haven't and we won't."

Muldoon nods. "It was different when the Major was alive," he says. "One thing Smythe loved was a good scrap."

"Yeah," beams Clancy. "If ye can't beat 'em out in the alley, ye won't beat 'em inside on the ice," Clancy quotes Smythe's famous phrase.

Clancy's presence and his endless enthusiasm takes Pat Muldoon's thoughts across the decades to the 1930s, when Clancy was a player and Smythe was in action and Foster Hewitt's matchless broadcasting style was making the Leafs the favourite hockey team of half the population of Canada. Muldoon is beginning to feel a whole lot better.

Early on in Muldoon's career at the *World,* he didn't know the shy and rather reclusive Hewitt very well, but Smythe was already an old comrade. A lad in his late teens, Muldoon had served in the Major's 30th Battery in France. Later, they occasionally went to the racetrack together. Muldoon knew that as a boy Smythe had gone there with his father and that by the late 1920s he owned a couple of horses. One was a two-year-old of no particular promise named Rare Jewel, a filly he'd bought for a mere $250. Rare Jewel had been nominated by a previous owner for a

stakes race, the Coronation Futurity. As a token of what
Smythe later called loyalty, he bet $40 on her with a down-
town bookmaker, though he was convinced privately that
Frothblower was the horse to beat in the Coronation.

Where had he read of the saga of Rare Jewel? Sure, in
the Smythe autobiography that Scott Young had put
together in 1981, the part about how on the day of the
Coronation, Smythe had lined up at Woodbine's betting
windows intent on putting $60 on Frothblower. There, he
was hailed by the district coroner, Dr. Smirle Lawson.
"Frothblower all the way, eh Connie?" chortled Lawson,
clapping Smythe's back.

In the book Smythe said he earlier fired Lawson as the
Maple Leafs team doctor "because he'd told a good game
guy with a broken leg that the leg wasn't broken, go out and
play." He told Lawson, "You might be all right as a coroner,
Smirle, but for the living you're a dead loss. You're fired."

So when Lawson clapped his shoulder and said what he
said, Smythe was annoyed and slapped down the money he
was going to bet on Frothblower and snapped, "Sixty
across on Rare Jewel!"

Of course, Rare Jewel won. In a monumental upset, her
betting payoff was $214.40 for each winning $2 ticket,
$46.75 for place and $19.95 for show. Smythe pocketed
between $10,000 and $11,000 for his bets at the track and
with the downtown bookmaker and an additional $3,570 as

the purse won by Rare Jewel. And this, of course, was the extra money he needed to pry King Clancy loose from the Senators.

In the coffee shop the two old-timers are silent, reflecting on that past glory. Clancy can see that recalling that far-off night has brightened Pat Muldoon's former baleful mood. He watches as the grizzled sports columnist strokes his heavy, pointed chin, his mind obviously many miles away. Muldoon is a tall man, thin and slouched, and he walks with a slow shuffle. A reputation he gained during the Second World War as the worst-dressed private soldier in the Canadian Army was not acquired overnight; he had been something less than immaculate before he went in and he'd not lost ground since. But his pen can charm the birds from the trees. Readers dote especially on the whimsical doggerel that often leads off his daily column in the Toronto *World*. Some people say Muldoon's stuff reminds them of Ted Reeve when Ted was the sage of the old Toronto *Telegram* on Melinda Street. Once, after Boston had beaten Toronto on an overtime goal by Bobby Bauer, Reeve had rhymed:

There was a young fellow named Bauer
Who let go a shot from afauer.
The puck hit the nets
With our six to five bets
And three payments we owe on our cauer.
(Pass the towel.)

Muldoon pines for the happy days of old when life moved more slowly and hockey players usually were local boys who grew up on the neighbourhood rinks and graduated to play for the Leafs. He knew that the famous Kid Line of the 1930s — Charlie Conacher on right wing beside the smooth gentleman Joe Primeau at centre and the brilliant brash left winger Busher Jackson — featured three hometown Toronto boys. Red Horner, who was Clancy's defence partner, was a local kid, and Hap Day, another defenceman, had played with the Toronto St. Patricks even before Connie Smythe bought that team and renamed it the Maple Leafs. Back then, nobody knew how much money guys were being paid. Or cared. Why, Clancy used to go into Smythe's office in the fall to sign his contract and Smythe would say to him, "What'll it be this year, King?" And Clancy would grin and tell him, "Whatever ye've got written in will do," and he'd sign the contract without even looking at the figure and know it was fair. Or think it was, anyway.

Another thing about the era, the Leafs were bringing a softer image to Toronto, a despised town in most of the country, or, at any rate, Foster Hewitt's broadcasts were. Fans across the prairies, where Toronto was reviled, sent letters by the bagful to Maple Leaf Gardens praising Hewitt.

No praise like that had happened for years. Now, with Ballard the boss, all that matters is money. Ticket prices have climbed up, up, up. New rows of seats have gone into the arena to replace the old wider ones and create less leg room, boosting the seating capacity. A well-worn joke is that Ballard takes the brush and a can of paint to the seats every fall, making more rows of cheap seats the colour of expensive ones.

Clancy reminds Muldoon that in Smythe's time there wasn't an advertisement anywhere in the building. Now ads are plastered everywhere.

"It was like a cathedral in here," Clancy says in wonderment that is typical of that sentimental man.

Muldoon is fully aware that Smythe was a martinet, but he has respect for the fact Smythe, at the height of the Depression in 1931, was the force behind the building of the Gardens. In its time it was the finest, cleanest, brightest arena on the continent. Indeed, Smythe made hockey so respectable in Toronto that it matched opera and ballet on the social scale. One time he wrote a form letter to box-seat season-ticket holders chiding them for a declining standard in dress. Muldoon wishes the steamy Gardens of today were as classy.

He misses the Old Man personally, too. These days, with the Maple Leafs stumbling and only Clancy showing enthusiasm in the old building, Muldoon regrets that Smythe's achievements are unknown to young hockey fans and have been forgotten by many old ones. Accordingly, when Smythe died on a November morning in 1980 at the age of 85, Muldoon wrote a piece about what the Old Man had accomplished: owned a horse, Jammed Lovely, who won the Queen's Plate; operated a hockey team that won the Stanley Cup seven times; became a prisoner of war and escaped twice; was caught twice; won the Military Cross; went to jail for slugging a Boston hockey fan; survived an airplane crash; stole a railroad locomotive; and caused a national crisis in his native land. The latter happened when Smythe lay wounded on a hospital ship returning from the Second World War and, risking a court-martial, charged that replacements in France were inadequate — untrained men were being sent into action because the Canadian government, bowing to Quebec's hatred of conscription, was refusing to send well-trained conscripted men overseas. In the uproar that ensued, the minister of national defence resigned.

"He was an outspoken man who most admired loyalty to himself and guts in others, perhaps not in that order," someone wrote. Many sportswriters quoted one of Smythe's favourite lines, "The difference between a hockey player and a football player or a baseball player is that hockey guys play if they can breathe." Muldoon recognizes that Smythe often was an irascible, arrogant, stubborn tyrant. But, still, he produced the brightest era in Maple Leaf history. In his time and for 30 years at the Gardens, he ruled with an iron fist.

Smythe wasn't a big fellow. He didn't rise much past Muldoon's stooped shoulders. But he was solidly built and until he was wounded at Caen, France, soon after D-day, he had kept himself in flat-bellied shape. He could he utterly charming — funny, expansive, warm and outgoing, with a sudden sunny smile, a merry twinkle in his pale blue eyes and a powerful quality of personality. And there was the other side, Muldoon knows, and he reminds Clancy that Smythe could shred people with a cold, impassive stare, the blue eyes suddenly round dimes of ice. It wasn't so much that he didn't speak to people, it was that they weren't even *there*.

"True enough, true enough," Clancy says uneasily. He is the sort of man who rarely speaks an unkind word about anyone.

Muldoon is benign enough, too, but now, in the Ballard era, he yearns for the prankish days of the legendary early Leaf teams. Hell, the players were like schoolboys, but there was a fellowship Muldoon doesn't perceive in modern teams. These days, players have agents — *agents,* for God's sake! — and make endorsements and don't really show much interest in one another.

Suddenly Muldoon chuckles, thinking about the time Baldy Cotton bought a new fedora and wore it climbing on the overnight train to Detroit, Michigan. Clancy and his running mate, Charlie Conacher, plotted how to aggravate Cotton. When a half-dozen players gathered for a card game in the smoker at the end of their sleeping car, Conacher got Cotton into the game while Clancy ducked out. Then

Clancy reappeared and stood behind Conacher wearing Cotton's new hat. But now the hat was out of shape and smudged. When Cotton saw it, his face grew red and he yelled, "You little bastard!" and lunged for Clancy, who fled while the players hooted. Then Clancy burst back into the room, still in Cotton's hat, except now it was clean and new. The players soon realized, and so did Cotton, that Conacher and Clancy had brought a battered old lid aboard with them.

Oh, hell, Muldoon thinks now, it was childish stuff. But it shows how hockey players then were less sophisticated, though a group together, a team. That's what Muldoon thinks is missing now.

And the memory of Baldy Cotton makes him think about another historic game, the night in Toronto when the Leafs played the second-longest game in hockey history — the 1933 semifinal against Boston that went into a sixth *overtime* period, the equivalent of just under three full games. There were no goals during the regulation three periods and the game was scoreless through the first 20-minute overtime period. There followed a second, a third, a fourth and even a fifth goalless overtime.

Along about midnight, Conn Smythe sent word to the young broadcaster, Foster Hewitt, to tell local radio listeners they could come down to the Gardens and see the rest of the game free. Night owls began to filter in. After 100 minutes of overtime, Smythe and Art Ross, the Boston general manager, asked the league president, Frank Calder, if they could stop play now and renew it the following night. No, they couldn't; the winner had to be in New York the next night to open the Stanley Cup final against the Rangers. Still, Smythe continued to put forward suggestions. "We could toss a coin," he said. Ross glared at him. "Don't be ridiculous," he snapped. "How about we remove the goaltenders?" Smythe offered. Ross fumed.

Muldoon once asked Smythe why he had made those dumb suggestions. "I figured with a little extra rest my players would be okay," Smythe said. "So I kept the conversation going."

After the discussion with Ross, Smythe went to the dressing room where the Leafs were sitting dispiritedly or lying on the floor. Cotton was one of those, looking like he'd never be able to get up. But Smythe had seen him in enough fights to know his spirit.

Smythe looked downcast. "They want to call the game," he told his team.

Suddenly alive, Cotton jumped to his feet. He'd taken off his skates. He was in his socks. "No son of a bitch is going to call *this* game," he shouted.

Other players also began showing signs of life.

"C'mon, ye bastards," yelped Clancy. "Let's kick ass."

They trooped to the ice, surprisingly spry considering the hour and their long ordeal. And, wouldn't you know, after four minutes and 46 seconds Andy Blair, a tall and scholarly fellow from Winnipeg, Manitoba, slipped a pass-out to Ken Doraty, a little blond winger from Regina, Saskatchewan, and Doraty put the puck past a diving Tiny Thompson in the Boston cage. Once again the Bruins were sidelined.

It was a high moment in Leaf history that Muldoon likes to reconstruct for visitors to the Toronto Press Club, where he takes his appetite for fellowship and Myers's rum every afternoon. There they sit, the regulars, telling stories and second-guessing coaches.

For the hard-living Muldoon, the afternoons often stretch long into night, and early the following morning he totters into the sports department at the *World* to write his daily piece. Sometimes he takes a pair of scissors to a newspaper from a disorderly pile that leans precariously on his desk amid empty soft drink bottles, glue pots, stubs of pencils, paper cups and an old overshoe. He carefully pastes a clipping from *The New York Times* to a sheet of copy paper, picks up one of the pencils and scrawls on the top of the clipping, "What does Red Smith mean by this?" and sends it off to the composing room. Other times when distressed by a hangover, he writes above one of his own old columns, "Repeated by Request." Then he shuffles off to the office of a guy named Del who runs the parking garage at the nearby King Edward Hotel. Del usually has a bottle of Myers's. This prepares Muldoon for the afternoon at the

Press Club where little Bob Sneath, the bartender, is ready for business at 11:30 most mornings (if Bob has had a good night).

As often as not in the afternoon, conversation turns to Connie Smythe.

Nursing his lukewarm coffee, Muldoon reflects that the famous old Gardens is Smythe's lasting legacy. It has been officially declared a historic building, meaning it can't be torn down or disfigured. Chances are, though, Muldoon reflects, the old place never would have grown into one of the country's landmarks had Smythe not insisted when the Gardens opened that Leaf games be broadcast. Of course, the Old Man had been lucky that a broadcaster of Foster Hewitt's unique style and ability showed up.

Once Muldoon asked Hewitt how his most enduring phrase, "He shoots! He scores!" had begun.

"It just happened," Hewitt said in his understated way. "There was nothing dramatic about it. It just seemed the easiest way to describe it."

The reply, Muldoon decides, was the essence of Hewitt. He never drew attention to himself or to his work. He never postured. If he'd had his way, he'd have always been in the background. He never uttered a pretentious syllable in his 83 years of life. But as the best broadcaster who ever sat down to describe a sport, he became a national institution.

And with that voice of his, that unique, spare style, he turned Maple Leaf Gardens into a tourist attraction as revered as any building in Canada. On many a morning when Muldoon shuffles to work along Front Street past Union Station, he knows outlanders are climbing from their berths aboard a transcontinental train hauling in from the West, and it is a rare morning when some one of them doesn't emerge from the depot, glance down from a quick inspection of the Royal York Hotel across the street and ask, "Say, how far is it to Maple Leaf Gardens?"

A reporter whose desk in the *World* sports department is not far from Muldoon's once told him what it was like growing up on the prairies and hearing that unmistakable voice on a Saturday night. "You'd be standing in front of the bathroom mirror shaving for a big date and the radio would be turned way up," the young man said. "You'd hear Foster greet us, 'Hello, Canada and hockey fans in the United States and Newfoundland,' and he'd always begin in that measured way of his, the tone verging on excitement. 'The score at the end of the first period...' And then he'd tell us, the millions of us spread clean across the country, people brought together in living rooms and kitchens and bathtubs and cars and on lonely dark farms and in small snow-packed towns and in big brightly lit cities from one ocean to the other, all of us in our mind's eye watching the matchless giants on the ice below. That was so long ago that the game was already a half-hour old before the broadcast came on, long before television."

As Hewitt's popularity grew, Muldoon was asked by the editor of *Maclean's* to write a 3,000-word profile on him. Accordingly, one night Muldoon joined Hewitt at the Gardens to observe his game-night routine. A half-hour before game time, they left Hewitt's narrow, picture-lined office on the third floor of the Gardens to begin a long, twisting trek to a catwalk high in the domed arena's rafters leading to an open booth Hewitt called his "gondola," a word that became accepted across the country.

Up there, Muldoon put away his notebook and carefully watched every step he took. Foster told him that George Raft, a movie gangster, had refused to go farther, and Muldoon believed it. Hewitt's father, the sports editor, had refused to go there. Conn Smythe had refused to go there. Even the seemingly fearless King Clancy, at the height of his popularity in the early 1930s, had refused to go to the gondola. "I'm crazy," Clancy laughs, recalling for Muldoon that night he was invited to join Hewitt, "but not that crazy."

Hewitt's occasional mention of his gondola made the booth almost as famous as the rink that contained it, so Muldoon, a man who respected tradition, was dismayed years later when the gondola had to be replaced by larger facilities to accommodate television's needs and the kindly old Gardens proprietor, Harold Ballard, had it torn down and junked, rather than shipped to the Hockey Hall of Fame, where it belonged.

Muldoon was just a boy when he first became aware of that gondola, and Clancy was growing a trifle long in the tooth for a hockey player. The game that is forever seared into Muldoon's brain involved the Leafs and the Bruins, when Clancy played what was perhaps the best game of his life.

So, with a twinkle in his eye, Muldoon leans across the table. "King," he says, "do you ever think of the night you made a monkey out of Eddie Shore?"

A smile breaks across Clancy's scarred old pan.

"Ah, c'mon Patrick," he says. "Ye know I'll never forget 1936. An' say, you'd be practically a babe in arms."

Well, not quite that young, Muldoon thinks, but, yes, he was only a boy growing up in Toronto, a Leaf fan of course. He used to listen to Hewitt on the radio and read everything he could find about the players. He had even taken scissors to a clipping about that game that a guy writing in the *Globe* had called the most sensational comeback in playoff history.

It was a semifinal playoff series with Boston — two games, total goals. It had begun poorly in Boston, a 3–0 loss there, and when the Bruins scored a first-period goal in the return match in Toronto, they had climbed into a four-goal advantage.

"Sure, I remember the night," Muldoon grins, looking at Clancy. "It was the night you sat on Charlie's knee."

Clancy's battered mug glows. On that long-ago night, trailing 4–0, he had edged himself into the dressing-room toilet for a smoke between periods. He sat on the toilet seat and lit up. Moments later Charlie Conacher, the big, gruff, goal-scoring star, pushed his way into the cubicle.

"Get up," he ordered Clancy.

"Fuck off," growled the King. "I'll not be gettin' up fer the likes o' you. You can't put the puck in the ocean."

Big Conacher placed his hands under Clancy's armpits and lifted him from the seat. He sat there himself and set Clancy on his lap.

"It's that Beattie," he grumbled. "He's on me like a tent. I'm surprised he's not in here now." Conacher meant Red Beattie, the Boston left winger, who was checking him.

Clancy brightened suddenly, an idea forming. "Look, what ye do, ye *immobilize* the son of a bitch,"

133

he said in mounting delight. "Let him skate close when I've got the puck an' when I pass it, you let him reach fer it. When he does, give him everything ye've got!"

"Are you crazy?" frowned Conacher. "If I get a penalty with us down 4–0, the Old Man will have my ass."

"What's there to lose?" Clancy reminded him. "Didn't ye just say it's four to nothin'?"

And so they went out for the second period and when Clancy got the puck, he whipped it toward Conacher and when Beattie reached for it, Conacher gave his red-headed cover a thorough facial massage using his fibre-covered left elbow and a few inches of the end of his stick. And the referee, a former player named Odie Cleghorn, either missed it or decided to ignore it. Moments later, the bruiser for the Toronto defence, Red Horner, scored a rare goal, getting the Leafs onto the scoreboard. The goal incensed Eddie Shore, the Bruins backbone defenceman, who insisted Cleghorn should disallow the goal because Horner had been in the goal crease. Cleghorn waved him away. Whereupon Clancy went into action. He tripped Shore and escaped without a call from Cleghorn. When Shore climbed to his feet, Clancy skated alongside and muttered, "My God, man, what's happenin'? The man's blind, Eddie. Red was in the crease, surer'n hell, an' he missed me tripping ye, didn't he, now?"

The puck lay near Shore's feet and he whacked it disgustedly in the general direction of Cleghorn. But it hit the referee squarely on the buttocks, a circumstance that drew Shore a two-minute penalty. Livid, the star defenceman picked up the puck and hurled it into the crowd. For that, he got an additional 10-minute misconduct penalty, and while he was away, the Leafs got back into the series. Pat Muldoon finds he is smiling to himself as he remembers that first Conacher scored, then Clancy, then big Conacher again to tie the series 4–4. The Bruins, even with Shore's return to the ice, were a dispirited bunch. The Leafs were exhilarated. They won the game 8–3 and the round 8–6, sending Shore and the Bruins out of the playoffs.

And the recollection of that long-ago night sends Muldoon into the dismal spring morning with something to write about. He'll remind the fans of better days. He'll do a flashback. He'll tell 'em again of Clancy's last hurrah.

CLANCY, FRANCIS (KING): Ottawa, Toronto — 1921–37

Regular Schedule

SEASONS	GP	G	A	TP	PIM
16	592	137	143	280	904

Playoff Schedule

GP	G	A	TP	PIM	CUP WINS
61	9	8	17	92	3

6

THE NEW YORK RANGERS

BY JEFF Z. KLEIN

Now I Can Die in Peace

"GRANDPA! LISTEN! LISTEN! THEY FINALLY DID IT!" HUH?
Yes, yes, I hear it now, the radio, the shouts, the chanting, the fireworks. They're playing it over and over on the radio: "That's one that will last a lifetime!"

You can turn that thing down, boy, I can hear it fine. It's great, let them have their fun. They deserve it, all the shit they took over the years.

Hell, *we* took. Wasn't I there for eons, suffering like everyone else? Dropping a bundle every year on tickets, long after those 400 games they played each season stopped meaning a single damn thing, then paying even more for the privilege of seeing them get shellacked in a couple of playoff games. But no! That's not the way to think — not tonight. Everyone is happy.

Go on, go and celebrate with your friends, go out into the city, go out and find the Cup, drink from it, boy, feel how cold it must be to the touch, feel how it transmits the temperature of whatever's in its bowl.

I guess the Curse is ended.

People say Red Dutton and his Amerks — that's what they called the New York Americans — cursed the Rangers so they'd never win another Stanley Cup, but I happen to know that's bullshit. That wasn't the Curse. I know what the Curse was. But first let me try to get my boy to go home.

Hey, go on now! I appreciate your coming out here at night, but you should really be with your friends, you should be out in the city, not in a goddamn cemetery holding a radio to a grave. Go on, get going, boy. Don't forget to put a pebble on my headstone on your way out.

Now … I'll tell you all about the Curse.

I was born in Brooklyn, out near Coney Island. In those days we really didn't have hockey, but by the time I got to be a teenager, we had roller hockey. We'd put on roller skates and go out to the parking field under the BMT and skate around for hours, shooting a spaldeen at goals we'd marked off with our jackets. We had a lot of yeshiva b'ruchas playing with us — my family wasn't observant, Yom Kippur, Rosh Hashanah, Pesach, shabbos candles, and that was pretty much it — but these other guys would come in with their yarmulkes and their payes and the white cotton strings hanging down below their belts, and one or two of them could really move, so they'd have all this stuff hanging off them, flying in the breeze as they wheeled around.

One time I was back on defence and one of these Lubavitchers comes peeling in on me. It's just me between him and the goal, and right at that moment the train starts screeching overhead on the el and all these sparks are raining down on us, and he's yelling something in Yiddish or Lithuanian or some damn thing, but I can't hear above the train, and he comes up just in front of me and all of a sudden, as I'm reaching to knock the ball off his stick, all of a sudden I see his hand come up and *pow,* next thing I know I'm on the pavement seeing stars. Holy shit! There's blood dribbling down my chin; I got brush burns on my elbows. And he comes rolling over, having just scored, and asks how I am. And I see this fucking yeshiva boy is wearing tefillin!

Okay, you may not know, but it's a little lacquered wooden box, filled with parchment, strapped onto the back of his hand, something used only by the most devout Jews for prayers — and this son of a bitch is not only playing hockey with one of these things on, but he uses it to knock me flat on my ass! Jesus Christ! Like he's reading the Talmud and he comes across a passage that says, "Rabbi Gamliel teaches that it is permissible to wear phylacteries only when praying or when standing upon wheels as did Elijah when he was borne up to heaven" and interpreting that to mean he can use it to belt someone while playing roller hockey. The kid probably grew up to be a great rabbi. But he was still an asshole.

Anyway, you can see how I came to like the game. I'd stand on line for tickets to the Rangers — never the Americans, who were a bunch of losers — and stand in the balcony at the old Madison Square Garden at 50th and Eighth. I couldn't see shit through all the cigar smoke that drifted up to the top of the building. But it didn't matter. You could still make out Ching Johnson because of the glare off the top of his bald head. One time when the Blackhawks were in, we used Johnson's head as a triangulation beacon to figure out where Charlie Gardiner was standing in the Chicago crease. Then we dropped heated pennies on him. We figured if we missed, at least we'd muck up the ice in front of his net. We couldn't see what happened through the haze, but I read in the next day's paper that Gardiner was hopping mad. Sputtered something about "haggis," as I recall.

A bit later, when I was 17, I lucked into a job as an office boy at the Garden through a friend of a cousin of mine who was an accountant there. Now you've got to realize that in those days sports wasn't the big deal it is today. It wasn't, "Oh my God, I'm going to be in close proximity to all my favourite heroes." You knew they were schmucks just like you. It was different if you were talking about Babe Ruth, Lou Gehrig, Joe DiMaggio, Joe Louis — those guys were royalty. But the Rangers? This was New York, where nobody gave a shit about hockey except the 10,000 or 12,000 who showed up for the games. I mean, these galoomps were *Canadians*, for Christ's sake. But I was glad to get the job.

In those days the Rangers were pretty good — in fact, only Boston was better. So you can imagine how happy everyone was in my second year on the job when, after we finished second to them in the standings again, we beat them in the first round of the playoffs. That meant we had to beat only one other team to win the Stanley Cup, which turned out to be the Toronto Maple Leafs. We won the first two games at the Garden, but then the series had to move to Toronto for the duration because, like every year, the circus came into New York and that was the Number 1 draw, so out the Rangers went, Cup final or no. As a lowly office boy, I didn't get to make the trip up north. But I was happy as hell when we won the Cup in six games. I'll never forget the date: April 13, 1940. An auspicious day, because that was also the day I went to see my doctor about a weird twinge I'd been getting in my chest, which had almost caused me to black out a couple of times. He told me it was my heart, and that I'd have to take a daily pill to keep the old ticker pumping or else it'd be coma time for me. And hey, said the doc, lighting up a Camel, how 'bout those Rangers?

A few months later, there am I in the executive suite, discharging my duties as gofer at a gathering of all the Garden suits standing around tuxedoed and acting august, the Madison Square Garden Corporation. You should have seen these guys. I mean, they couldn't be serious. But they were. There was a guy named Hamilton Bail, a Jansen Noyles, Bernard Gimbel of department-store fame and, of course, the Garden president, General John Reed Kilpatrick. All these distinguished officers of the corporation, these captains of commerce in black tie, and the centrepiece at the table of honour is the Stanley Cup itself.

"Gentlemen," Kilpatrick harrumphs like he's the King of New York Sportsmen and these are his dukes and viscounts, "we have a most happy task to perform this day. For today we pluck the fruits our efforts have borne, fruits sprung from seeds planted 20 years ago, when a group of investors — including several of us presently gathered here in this room — decided that our metropolis should have a new Madison Square Garden. An entertainment palace in the finest traditions of all the previous Madison Square Gardens, but bigger, better, more! Boxing, circuses, hockey, figure skating, dog shows, horse shows, even basketball, all for the enjoyment of the people of this great city in this young giant of a nation. I daresay, and I don't mean to minimize this fact, that we investors have been amply recompensed for our shrewd investment and judicious management of this enterprise. That is the nature of capital, regardless of what Mr. Roosevelt might say, eh Noyles?" — manly laughter all around — "and it has worked for the good of all, even during the difficult years of the Depression, which God willing is finally behind us."

I'm wondering what's his point already, but all the other execs are looking up at the General, smiling smugly, like they've got hours to kill before their tee time at Winged Foot and all the Scotch and sodas in the world to drink while they're waiting. "You see before you the Stanley Cup, emblematic of hockey supremacy," continues the General, coining a phrase. "And here, in my hand," he says, reaching into his tux and producing a neatly folded, slightly yellowed document from the inside breast pocket, "you see the mortgage to this building. Three million dollars. Last Friday, as you know, this corporation made the last payment on this mortgage" — at which the tuxes all start to applaud and emit self-satisfied shouts of "Bravo!" and "Here, here!" till the grinning Kilpatrick, strapping and red-faced with athletic vigour, finally holds up one hand to get them to simmer down — "rendering…rendering this piece of paper utterly useless. Well! What shall we do with it? Why, what everyone does when they pay off a mortgage — they *burn* it! And so shall we!"

"Excellent!"

"Yes! Burn it! That's the ticket!"

"Gentlemen! *Gentlemen!* Please! This is a place of *business*. Let's not devolve into a mob of frenzied yahoos at this juncture, what with representatives of the press on hand to witness this happy occasion. Now then, I believe you were assenting to my proposal that we *burn* this mortgage?"

"Yes!"

"Then burn it we shall! The motion, I daresay, is carried. Therefore, I believe the next order of business is to place the mortgage in an appropriate receptacle, one suitable for its ignition and complete immolation. Ah, I believe this Stanley Cup here will do quite nicely. Yes?"

"Brilliant! Burn it in the Stanley Cup!"

I was horrified. Was the General really going to defile the Cup by burning some financial document in it? I had seen how hard the players had worked to win that thing, how they'd laughed as they hugged it and drank out of it, how reverently Frankie Boucher and Lester Patrick, the coach and manager, who'd bled for the Cup so many times as players, gazed upon it in the dressing room, how all those Canucks up in Toronto got all hot about the funny-looking silver stovepipe with all the names on it, this trophy that was *almost 50 years old,* for Christ's sake! And Kilpatrick was going to *burn* something in it?

"Now to secure a *match.* For this, I turn to my distinguished Garden staff... Boy, bring us a match, will you?"

He was looking right at me, his eyes sparkling with the unmistakable glint of a jolly steel knife blade. If I didn't produce a match pronto, I got the distinct impression, I'd be better off serving the interests of the Madison Square Garden Corporation somewhere in London as, say, a decoy target for Luftwaffe bombers. So I fumbled through my pockets and came up with a box of matches, but I still felt queasy about the whole thing.

"Boy? What are you waiting for? Don't hold up the proceedings. Or would you like to continue paying off the interest rate on this mortgage out of your salary?"

General hilarity all around. I felt my face redden as the guffaws failed to subside, and, thus shamed, I stepped forward. It took 13 strides to make my way over to where Kilpatrick was standing and hand him the matchbox and that single, blasphemous matchstick — 13 ruinous steps that changed my life, the lives of everyone present, and the lives of millions of New Yorkers who never could have guessed at the existence of the people in that room, chewing on cigars, sipping champagne from fluted glasses, visualizing the silk-sheathed legs of their chorine mistresses curling round that tall, shiny, upright shaft of a thing.

"Thank you, my young friend. And now, step back, if you will, so that everyone here can get a good look at what I'm about to do. Can the photographers get a clear shot of this? Fine. Gentlemen, as I strike this match" — with a flourish, he struck sulphur to flint and held the small, implacable flame just over the paper-stuffed bowl of the venerable trophy — "I congratulate us once more on seeing this noble enterprise through to this landmark moment. To our continued success!"

"Here, here!"

Kilpatrick lowered the match and ignited the document. It caught instantly, and the flame rose up what seemed like two feet before I turned away, unable to watch the profaning of this beloved urn, now transformed into a furnace, a hecatomb for the lucre-drenched schemes of these rich men. The room fell silent, and my averted gaze fell across the faces of the other shareholders present, the firelight reflecting crimson in their wide eyes, the glow of the flames dancing in the depths of the zircon studs on their shirtfronts. They stood, mouths open, champagne glasses in hand, the ends of their cigars glowing well clear of their polished and neatly cuticled fingernails, enjoying this, the payoff for their avarice, an indoor bonfire that used as a prop an object fought and bled over by scores of working-class foreigners — a wealth-confirming, status-enhancing potlatch, but one in which someone else's hard-earned capital gets pissed away. Like I said, sports wasn't such a big deal in those days, but even then I knew there was something really, really wrong about burning something in the Stanley Cup.

And I knew I wasn't the only one who felt that way when, the next day, I was asked to bring some sheet music to Lester Patrick.

"Here you are, Mr. Patrick," I announced respectfully as I entered his office. "The latest Cole Porter."

"Thank you, my lad," said the Silver Fox, fixing that suave gaze of his on me, one eyebrow slightly raised, his head almost imperceptibly cocked to one side, the corners of his mouth fixed level, yet one of them suggesting the imminent, or at least eventual, emergence of a wry smile. "Tell me, son, were you present at yesterday's ceremony in this corporation's executive offices?"

"I was, sir."

"And did you witness what went on there? Are the newspaper reports correct? Was there *actually* a fire set in the Stanley Cup itself?"

"Yes, there was, Mr. Patrick, sir."

"Oh dear. How could they have done such a thing?"

You have to understand that Lester Patrick spoke with such understated concision, such perfect politesse, that when he said something like that, the actual meaning of his words carried roughly 200 times more gravitas, like the government of a world power expressing "consternation" over "an apparent impasse" with a small republic two days before carpet-bombing its capital. No longer was there any suggestion of a smile on Patrick's narrow, granite face. Instead I thought I saw a look of accusation in it, but of course that was only my own sense of guilt welling up inside me. After a moment's reflection, during which the great man must have visited the infernal scene of horror in his own mind, the flames licking at the Cup's delicate patina, the staining and blackening of the goblet's silvery sheen, the vaporizing of the tears and sweat of those who died that we might drink from its hallowed confines, he looked up at me again and asked, quietly, "Did you do anything to stop it?"

I was crushed by the question, the full weight of my complicity bearing down on me like a great granite slab, which is ironic considering my present circumstances.

"No, sir."

"No, I don't suppose you could have, could you?" I didn't tell him about the match.

Can you fathom what the rest of my life was like after

that incident? Again, I have to stress that sports was not the alpha and omega of my concerns. I stayed at the Garden job for about another year, until Pearl Harbor. Then I went off to the war, which I spent in the Pacific island-hopping with the Army — at least we were smart enough to go in after several days' bombardment, unlike the Marines, who walked in first thing and got slaughtered in bunches, but you meet some of those assholes here and they're still proud of themselves, like it's a great achievement to get your face blown off "for the Corps." That was just the fucking war.

Then I came back, found a girl, got married, got a job, settled down, raised a daughter, lived life for another 45 years with all the tsuris that entails, and let me tell you, your interest in hockey tends to pale against so vast a panoply as an actual *life*, if you know what I mean. So many things to regret — an affair you had, an affair you didn't have, the fact that you only had one affair in all those years — so many things to rejoice in — my wonderful daughter, my darling grandson, the installation of air-conditioning in the subways — and *still*, the thing that would not go away, that nagging little harpie in my mind, this idea that somehow I was responsible for what, with time, came to be known as the Curse.

Rationally, I knew it was stupid. Subrationally, I knew it was true, but I could still dismiss it. So what? I figured. So I did something that meant some stupid hockey team would never win some stupid trophy in a sport that only about three million people in the world cared about anyway. This was not the Rosenbergs. This was not Khrushchev vowing to bury us (I wonder why I thought of that?). This was not Kissinger bombing Cambodia, Reagan ruining the country, the fall of Communism. I'm trying to think of something in case you're Canadian... This was not Meech Lake. What I'm saying is that it's only a hockey team. Who really gives a shit, right?

Well, I still got season tickets and would go to the games, even after they moved into that awful round thing the corporation built on the ruins of Penn Station, and I yelled as hard as anyone. I always figured that if they'd win the Cup, I'd be off the hook. But every year, they found some new way to lose. Jesus, some of the players they had! Billy Moe, Louie Fontinato, Dean Talafous, Eddie Mio, the Smurfs... my God, the things we put up with. And when they traded Jean Ratelle and Brad Park for Phil Esposito and the rest of those Bruin jerks, and the way they treated Ed Giacomin — don't get me started already. But there were nice people up there in the stands with us, even if I wound up with a core group of two dozen close friends whose common interest was the spontaneous composition of songs celebrating the presence of active pedophiles on the roster of the Washington Capitals. I guess you could

say this is the very definition of a wasted life, but I found it fulfilling.

Still, the belief that I was largely responsible for the Rangers' predicament would not go away. With each passing, futile season, my friends became more bitter, more ingeniously repulsive, more drunk with their own bile. So did the whole building full of Ranger fans. Eighteen thousand throats, screaming as one at the Rangers' foes, urging them to die behind the wheel of a sports car, reminding them that they were involved in a statutory rape scandal, ridiculing them because their ex-wives had accused them of spousal abuse in a divorce case, telling them over and over and over again that they *suck,* all roaring the earsplitting roar of frustration and dread and hate. It sounded great, but the guilt was starting to get me down. What were these people turning into? What was I turning into?

In 1985 I started going to the games with my grandson, my only grandchild, the little boy of my only child. He was only six, but he was already all cockeyed over the Rangers. My wife had stopped coming to games with me by then — in fact, besides filing a joint tax return once a year, she and I had pretty much stopped doing everything by then — so it wasn't long before I was taking my grandson to just about every game. He'd be all bright and cheerful in that manner that little kids have of rooting at sports events, yelling, "C'mon Rangers!" like he was watching a Saturday-morning cartoon hero and the good guy would always end up winning. Meanwhile, everyone else around him, me included, is howling for Nick Fotiu or Chris Nilan or whichever goon we happened to have up that week to *beat the shit out of that pussy.* Rhythmically. A thousand of us. Then the next section would take up the chant. I started to feel a little weird about my grandson hearing this kind of stuff, but it didn't seem to have any effect on him. At least not at first.

Pretty soon it got so that going to Ranger games with my grandson was all I really had to look forward to, once

☆ THE NEW YORK RANGERS ☆

I'd retired from my job, which was nothing to write home about anyway. I spent most days lounging around the house reading the *Times, Daily News, Post* and *Newsday,* in that order, before moving on to *Newsweek, Commentary, National Geographic,* the Bloomingdale's catalogue, the store circular for Food Emporium, my wife's copy of *Cat Fancy,* a stray edition of *The Atheist, Speculum World, American Lint,* whatever was lying around. Sure, you can say I was well read, but the important thing was the hockey with my grandson, who had just run out of immediate male family members when his father blew town without a word, leaving two months' worth of rent in the bank account and no forwarding address. To cushion the blow, I began calling him every day, and we'd talk about the Rangers for an hour or so before my daughter would cut us off by getting on the phone and making weak jokes about John Vanbiesbrouck not having to eat government cheese.

Everything was fine for a couple of years. Then one night my grandson and I are at a Rangers–Penguins game, and Mario Lemieux, who'd already scored his obligatory hat trick by the 30-second mark of the first period, now goes down in a heap after some Broadway Blue breathed on him in the neutral zone. Naturally, everyone in the stands starts the Asshole chant, but rising above it, piercing the air in a blaring alto, comes a voice so loud, so commanding, spewing filth so vile that everyone, and I mean *everyone,* in the Garden falls silent in terrified, revolted amazement: "You fucking turd, Lemieux! You shit-eating faker, you piece of waste!"

It is my grandson, all of 10 years old, standing atop his seat, a torrent of hate gushing forth from his distorted mouth.

"Take your fucking finger out of your ass, Lemieux, and stuff it down your throat and choke on it and die!"

Can this really be my little grandson? I watch in horror and shame, but I can't take my eyes off him, nor can I lift a finger to gesture at him to quiet down. I see that everyone in the building is looking at him in mute, scandalized wonder. And then I see that the boy notices that everyone is watching him. His eyes sparkle. He starts to chant: "Choke and die! Choke and die! Choke and die! *Come on, everybody!* Choke and die! Choke and die! Choke and die!"

Not even the Ranger fans picked up that one. They just stood there, awestruck, as if this kid were something irretrievably…else. The *echt* Ranger fan. A monster.

Was this the same sweet little boy I held as a baby? The same little boy for whom I'd been the only male elder for the last four years? The last thing in my long, reasonably eventful life that really mattered to me any more? What had I done to turn him into this child-prodigy frothing lunatic? I sat there thinking: Ranger fans didn't used to be spite-crazed maniacs, but I turned them into exactly that when I offered up the fateful match that profaned the Cup and doomed it from ever returning to the Garden. Now look at what I've done to my little boy. I sat there thinking these things. Meanwhile, my grandson was throwing heated pennies over the edge of the balcony.

He only got worse after that. When Pat LaFontaine of the Islanders got knocked unconscious during a playoff game and was carried off the ice with a possible spinal injury, he was among the doughty faithful who sneaked downstairs to rock the ambulance. When the Rangers acquired Tie Domi from Toronto, he showed up for games with "Kill, Domi, Kill!" painted on his face. When Joey Kocur came over from Detroit, he took to riding the Broadway local with his fists packed in huge wads of raw hamburger meat in mimetic tribute to the newest Blueshirt. One afternoon this past fall I was home reading the new issue of *Gastroenterology Illustrated* when the phone rang. It was my daughter.

"What are you doing right now?"

"I'm reading."

"Not any more you're not. You're going to help your grandson, right now."

"You help him. You're his mother."

"No way, Mr. Hockey Man. *You're* going to go fetch him. And you're going to take a little ride to New Jersey to do it."

"What?"

"He's in Mahwah. At the police station."

"What?"

"He's being held there on disorderly conduct charges, Mr. The-family-that-goes-to-Ranger-games-together-stays-together. He needs a relative to come get him, and I'll be goddamned if I'm going to humiliate myself by dealing with all the cops' questions and the family welfare questions, and me having to tell them about the lifesize Islander effigy hanging in his room, the beef shank bones laid out before the shrine to Ulf Nilsson, the…"

"Aw, come on. He's just an average Ranger fan."

"Fuck you, Dad. The average Ranger fan doesn't take a PATH train over to Jersey to bust up every plate-glass window on some little town's main street with a two-by-four screaming, 'Devils suck, Devils suck.' It took three cops to restrain him. It's a good thing they didn't shoot him."

"Jesus."

"Is that all you've got to say? 'Jesus'? Fuck you, Dad. He's your mess. You clean him up. And you'd better, or else it's no more hockey games, no more you screaming obscenities about hitting and hurting and losing and betrayal while sitting next to an impressionable young boy, my son, your *grandson*. In fact, I'll never let you see him again."

Well, that sealed it: the situation with my grandson had reached a crisis state, a suspicion that was confirmed when I met him at the Mahwah police station. He was shirtless, his chest painted white with red and blue piping, the letters R-A-N-G-E-R-S descending diagonally from right shoulder to left hip, his face painted with a little blue Empire State Building in emulation of John Davidson's classic goalie mask. He threw out his arms, as if to say, "What do you think of this getup — pretty cool, huh?" But before he could speak, I told him that this time he'd gone too far. We rode back to New York in silence, me feeling that old familiar twinge beneath my rib cage the whole way. I think he could tell I was disappointed in him; it seemed to make him a bit sheepish. On the other hand, maybe it was just that the angel dust wore off, or the hormones, or whatever it was that had made him act this way in broad daylight.

I dropped him off at his home, where I received a much-anticipated cool reception from my daughter, then I went to a diner to sit with a cup of coffee and try to think of a way to set my grandson straight. How could I put things right? I sat and I sat, unable to figure it out. Past twilight and deep into the night I sat there and thought, through countless cups of coffee and 14 trips to the bathroom — but on the 15th, I hit on a plan.

I went home immediately and set it in motion. First, I knocked on my wife's bedroom door, walked in and told her she was a good woman. You should have seen the look on her face — I had no idea one individual eyebrow could be elevated so much higher than the other. After dismissing myself with a minimum of further attention-drawing fuss, I went back to my room and got on the phone to my grandson. "Boy," I told him, "I want the Rangers to win as much as you do, but there's a certain line you just can't cross or else you turn into some kind of nut case. Sure, I know I set a rotten example. I say certain things at games, maybe some things it isn't seemly for a man my age to say — but you don't see me walking around smashing windows, do you?"

He was quiet on the other end of the phone. I continued, "Look, don't make your mother ashamed of you. You're all she's got." Finally my grandson spoke. "I know," he said.

"Let me make a deal with you, boy. Let's say right now that if anything happens to me, you get my season tickets, okay? But on two conditions: one, you've got to promise to keep yourself under control. Promise?"

"I promise."

"And two, you've got to take your mother with you to all the games."

"Aw, come on, Grandpa, that's ridiculous."

"You don't bring your mother, the deal's off. You do bring her, and everything will be fine. You make these promises to me, and I promise you that you'll be rewarded with something you want very much. And so will I."

Silence on the other end. "Deal?" I asked.

"I promise," he answered.

"Great," I said. "Did I ever tell you about the time Lester Patrick met Gershwin?" We talked on and on for quite a while, me telling him all about Frankie Boucher and General Kilpatrick and 1940 — leaving out one significant story, of course — and about playing roller hockey under the el in Brooklyn. It got very late, till finally I had to say goodnight. "Time for me to go, boy," I said. "You're going to be fine. I know it."

"Goodnight, Grandpa," he said, half-asleep himself.

Then I went to the medicine cabinet and took out my bottle of pills. Fifty-four years I've been taking these things, I thought. Never missed a day. Till now. And I poured them down the toilet, already feeling tired. I remember getting into bed and having a dream. I was holding my grandson when he was a little baby, just a couple of weeks old. He was looking up at me and smiling.

The next thing I remember I was here, meeting all these people, catching up on old friends, listening to the radio from up above, hearing the jubilation in the Garden, the players skating the Cup round the ice, some guy in the stands holding up a sign saying Now I Can Die In Peace, the announcer telling us how this will last a lifetime, all the frustration and bitterness and hate gone at last, replaced by relief and joy and love. I guess the Curse is lifted now, which will really upset old Red Dutton when he finds out, just like it'll make Lester and the General feel swell. They may have already heard, but I don't think they have the type of relatives who put transistor radios on top of graves. I do: my grandson, and I know he's going to be okay — unless the Devils win the Cup some day. Fat chance of that happening any time soon.

Yeah, I can see him now, taking the train back into the city, finding that old silver tankard in some wee-hours tavern teeming with celebrants. He smiles, he laughs, maybe he thinks of me for a moment, and then he grasps the Cup while a drunken Ranger holds it up high, letting him drink long and deep from that cool, shimmering bowl. Go on, boy. Go find your friends. Put a pebble on my headstone, and go into the city and celebrate.

*The Stanley Cup, some of you may recall, was won
the following year by New Jersey. — Ed.*